HABITS OF POETRY;
HABITS OF RESURRECTION

BENIGNO SANCHEZ-EPPLER

HABITS OF POETRY;
HABITS OF RESURRECTION

The presence of Juan Ramón Jiménez
in the work of Eugenio Florit,
José Lezama Lima and Cintio Vitier

TAMESIS BOOKS LIMITED

LONDON

Colección Támesis
SERIE A - MONOGRAFIAS, CXXV

DISTRIBUTORS:

Spain:
  Editorial Castalia,
  Zurbano, 39,
  28010 Madrid

United States and Canada:
  Longwood Publishing Group,
  27 South Main Street,
  Wolfeboro, New Hampshire 03894-2069, U.S.A.

Great Britain and rest of the world:
  Grant and Cutler Ltd.,
  55-57 Great Marlborough Street,
  London W1V 2AY

Depósito legal: M. 43018-1986

Printed in Spain by Talleres Gráficos de SELECCIONES GRÁFICAS
Carretera de Irún, km. 11,500 - 28049 Madrid

for
TAMESIS BOOKS LIMITED
LONDON

to all those involved
in making it possible
for me to study these habits
while indulging in others

especially

to my mistress of habits
with whom and for whom
all habits are studied
and indulged in

«... como el elefante,
lento,
pero aplastante.»

Cuban transcription of

«Wie das Gestirn,
Ohne Hast,
Aber ohne Rast.»

TABLE OF CONTENTS

		PAGE
ACKNOWLEDGEMENTS … … … … … … … … … … … … … … …		11
INTRODUCTION: THE MASTER OF NOVICES … … … … … … … … …		13
I.	SEEING, SAYING, AND SALVAGING IN THE POETRY OF JUAN RAMÓN JIMÉNEZ … … … … … … … … … … … … … … …	19
II.	JUAN RAMÓN IN PUERTO RICO (1936): «Mano amiga» … … …	26
III.	EUGENIO FLORIT AND THE MASTER: THE WEIGHT OF AN INFLUENCE … … … … … … … … … … … … … … … … …	29
IV.	COLLOQUY WITH JOSÉ LEZAMA LIMA … … … … … … … …	40
V.	THE EXAMINATION OF CINTIO VITIER … … … … … … … …	51
VI.	JUAN RAMÓN AFTER 1936: «Camino mundo arriba» … … …	56
VII.	FLORIT AFTER 1939: «Un hombre desvalido y solo» … … … …	62
VIII.	LEZAMA AFTER 1939: «La sustancia de lo inexistente» … …	69
IX.	VITIER AFTER 1939: «De la … poesía a la … conciencia» …	73
CONCLUSION: HABITS OF CREATION … … … … … … … … … …		85
LIST OF WORKS CONSULTED … … … … … … … … … … … …		91

ACKNOWLEDGEMENTS

My parents, who have always given me their love and support, as well as Spanish for a language and things Cuban for a home, remain the first providers of all those opportunities that brought me to the brink of the concerns explored in this study. My thanks are also due to all those in Williams College, Massachusetts who nursed my undergraduate enthusiasms, and who, assisted by the generosity of Dr Herchel Smith, lovingly dared to finance my first two years of study in England.

More specifically in relation to the work at hand, I am pleased to acknowledge that its publication was made possible by a generous grant from the Master and Fellows of Emmanuel College, Cambridge. I am also very grateful to Professors J. E. Varey, Paul Olson and Graciela Palau de Nemes whose careful review of the typescript during its final stages provided the advice which enabled me to turn a learner's tesina into this monograph. This study was presented as an M. Phil. dissertation at the University of Cambridge, where Emmanuel College, the Jebb Studentship Committee and the Centre of Latin American Studies jointly offered me the financial and institutional support necessary to survive my year of research and writing. My thanks go to them, to the Spanish Faculty, and to my graduate colleagues who harboured me, taught me and tolerated my excesses. From among these, I remain especially indebted to Lorna Close, for so many things as well as for my most substantial encounters with the canon of Spanish poetry; and to Alison Sinclair, for her hard work as supervisor of my research, for providing the handrails I needed to make chapters out of hints and guesses, and for her exemplary habits of productivity and sanity.

Yet to Karen, to whom my work is dedicated, and with whom I read and write...

BENIGNO SÁNCHEZ-EPPLER

Cambridge, July 1985.

11

INTRODUCTION

THE MASTER OF NOVICES

Sí, la poesía es actividad práctica.
Y el poeta es mucho más útil que el religioso,
por ej., porque lo que intenta el poeta es crear,
«aquí, ahora, y gratuitamente» la eternidad con la
belleza que el religioso pretende encontrar «allí,
luego, y como mérito».

(JRJ, *Orígenes*, no. 10, p. 3.)

A Master of Novices carries the overwhelming responsibility of introducing new monks to ways and means of dealing with the demands of their vocation and their new life. A Master of Novices teaches individuals, who have surrendered to their discipleship on their own, individually tuned ways and means of becoming monks. It can be argued that he discharges this responsibility by engaging the individual novice in a vital, non-academic curriculum that concentrates about one third of the efforts towards focusing on the aims of this becoming, and about another third towards discussing all the processes involved in this becoming. The final third of the vital engagement facilitated by the Master of Novices, amounts to the incorporation of those formulated and discussed aims and processes in the very flesh of each of the novices, and therefore in every manifestation of their richer habit of loving and their newest habit of living. To achieve the culmination of this curriculum, the monastery depends, most of all, on the way in which the novice chooses to emulate the love and life of all good monks present in the tradition as well as in the community. Viewed in these terms, the Master of Novices becomes no more than the most accessible among the many lovingly followed examples of how to dwell in the habits.

Juan Ramón Jiménez stands as the tallest Master of Novices within the community of Hispanic poets of the first half of the twentieth century, on both sides of the Atlantic. He practised his poetic vocation as rigorously as any other great poet within any other poetic community. He practised his vocation so thoroughly that one must agree with those

13

who praise his total surrender as all-inclusive and impeccable, as well as with those who criticise his all-consuming obsession as self-absorbing and misanthropic. His contacts with novices in Spain before his departure in August of 1936 has been widely acknowledged and studied as an important part of the cluster of formative experiences shared by a whole generation of first-rate poets. His contact with young poets in America, both through his *Obra* and through his visitations, is now demanding increased attention.

During Juan Ramón's visit to Cuba, between November 1936 and January 1939, his contacts with poets, critics, publishers and others were many and varied. For instance, Enrique and Dulce María Loynaz, and Serafina Núñez, were, like Eugenio Florit, subjects of Juan Ramón's lyrical portraits in *Españoles de tres mundos*. Fernando Ortiz, José María Chacón y Calvo, and Camila Henríquez Ureña, in their capacity as directors of the Institución Hispanocubana de Cultura, collaborated with Jiménez in the selection and publication of the anthology *La poesía cubana en 1936,* and made possible a number of lectures, poetry readings, and other public engagements before the kind of audiences which the recluse Juan Ramón had always managed to avoid until then. José Zacarías Tallet, Juan Marinello, Nicolás Guillén, Mariano Brull, and Emilio Ballagas, who already enjoyed the status of recognised poets, exercised, in their various ways, the role of welcoming poetic peers; for instance, by responding to Juan Ramón's initiative making their poems of 1936 available to be published in the already mentioned anthology, together with the efforts of younger or completely unknown talents. These new poets, including José Lezama Lima as well as Samuel Feijoo, Angel Gaztelu, Virgilio Piñera, Gastón Baquero, and Eliseo Diego, all remember the visit, the lectures, the presence of Juan Ramón in Cuba, as the principal cultural landmark of their early years of artistic endeavour. In fact, more than the contributions of the recognised older generation, it was the first poems of many of these younger poets, first published in *La poesía cubana en 1936,* that earned for the collection the rubric of «el granero». In one assertive exercise of his prerogatives as visiting master, Juan Ramón, as early as 1936, identified and championed the poets that would make the most significant contributions to Cuban poetry during the 1940s and the 1950s. In this respect, the young Cuban collaborators of *Orígenes* (1944-1956) owe as much to Juan Ramón as those young luminaries who first published in Juan Ramón's *Indice* in the Spain of the 1920s.

In the year of the centenary celebrations of the master's birth, two articles appeared in Spain demanding a detailed study of the contacts between Juan Ramón and the Caribbean poets with whom he talked and worked during his stay in Cuba and Puerto Rico. In these articles, Aurora de Albornoz[1] and Alberto Baeza Flores[2] both depend on Graciela

Palau de Nemes's account of the visit, as it appears in the chapter entitled «Puerto Rico y Cuba. Juan Ramón alienta juventudes» of her ground-breaking biographical study[3]. By the end of the centenary celebrations, other accounts of the visit and its impact were available, but they represent the *testimonios* of those with whom he came into contact, a record of impressions which might serve as useful guides to the events and the concerns shared, but that do not pretend to be a detailed study[4]. Also during 1981, Arcadio Díaz Quiñones and Raquel Sárraga released a collection of the vignettes Juan Ramón had written in, or about, Puerto Rico. In his introduction, Díaz Quiñones does discuss in some detail Lezama's «Coloquio con Juan Ramón Jiménez», as well as some aspects of Vitier's relationship with the Spanish master, but his emphasis remains focused on the task of prefacing a book essentially about Puerto Rico.[5] Another specifically Puertorican contribution to the celebrations appeared as a special issue of *Revista Sin Nombre*. This «Homenaje a Juan Ramón Jiménez» contained, among many others, a piece by Vitier described as the first chapter of his then recently published book *Juan Ramón Jiménez en Cuba*.[6] I was still researching and writing this study when the special issue of *Sin Nombre* fell into my hands; and then I had to wait a long time before I could see the whole of Vitier's latest contribution. To judge by its first chapter, the work promised to be the much needed in-depth book-length study, but it was not. It turned out to be something equally useful, namely a compilation of most of the material which I had to dig out from rather dispersed sources in libraries and magazine collections both in England and the United States. Thanks to the editorial efforts of Cintio Vitier, much of what Juan Ramón said during this singular period of his career, and much of what was said about him, and about the importance of his presence in Cuba, is now recorded in one volume.

By now most of the strictly historical documentation of Juan Ramón's contacts in the Americas, and particularly in the Caribbean, has been

---

[1] AURORA DE ALBORNOZ, «JRJ. Cuba. José Lezama Lima y otros poetas cubanos», *Insula*, 36, nos. 416-417 (July-August 1981), p. 7.

[2] ALBERTO BAEZA FLORES, «Juan Ramón Jiménez y las Antillas Mayores», *Cuadernos Hispanoamericanos*, nos. 376-378 (1981), pp. 64-80.

[3] GRACIELA PALAU DE NEMES, *Vida y obra de Juan Ramón Jiménez* (Madrid, 1957), pp. 293-301.

[4] Cf. GASTÓN BAQUERO, «Juan Ramón vivo en el recuerdo», *Cuadernos Hispanoamericanos*, nos. 376-378 (1981), pp. 81-89. See also the *encuesta* answered by LEZAMA, VITIER, and FINA GARCÍA MARRUZ, «El momento cubano de Juan Ramón Jiménez», *La Gaceta de Cuba*, no. 77 (October 1969), pp. 8-10.

[5] *Isla de la simpatía* (Río Piedras, 1981), pp. 11-29.

[6] CINTIO VITIER, «Juan Ramón Jiménez en Cuba», *Revista Sin Nombre*, 12, no. 3 (1982), pp. 31-56; reproduction of the «Prólogo» to *Juan Ramón Jiménez en Cuba* (La Habana, 1981), pp. 5-28. The piece is dated «Febrero 1980».

made available. This presentation concentrates its attention on texts, issues and traces that manifest the nature of the dialogue between the Spanish master, and only three of the young Cuban poets who came to him for that enriching combination of challenges and guidance and exchanges.

Whenever Eugenio Florit (1903-), José Lezama Lima (1910-1976), or Cintio Vitier (1921-) refer to Juan Ramón Jiménez, all their *testimonios* amount to *homenajes.* Their repeatedly-expressed enthusiasm in this respect clearly demonstrates the degree to which the Spanish poet fulfilled for these Cuban writers the role of the most convincing and accessible among the many lovingly followed examples of how to dwell in the habits of poetry.

To trace and document what they actually learned from him, gem by gem, to figure out which specific aims they formulated under his direction, or which specific processes they discussed during his *tertulias,* would send this investigation after the narrow and potentially tendentious scent of influences, whilst the intent is to center it, more broadly, on the pursuit of confluences. The term «confluence» is to be used in this study in its widest possible application. This exploration of shared concerns and their subsequent divergent development aims to arrive at a better understanding of those concerns, rather than at a definitive documentation of the facts of Juan Ramón's relationship with the three Cuban poets at hand. The story of the specific contacts among the poets will occupy an important place in my discussion, but not a central one.

What is the justification for choosing only three poets from among all those who enjoyed Juan Ramón's company during his Cuban interlude between November 1936 and January 1939? The choice is easier and less arbitrary than one would at first think. Florit's association with Juan Ramón has always been acknowledged, and the evidence of their contacts ranges from Juan Ramón's enthusiastic prologue written for Florit's *Doble acento* in 1937, to Florit's editorial participation in the publication of Juan Ramón's *Tercera Antolojía Poética* in 1957. Lezama's *tour de force* in his «Coloquio con Juan Ramón Jiménez» would be enough to merit his place among the many who ever held a fruitful dialogue with the Nobel laureate. This fictional reconstruction of Jiménez's voice was compelling enough to elicit the following endorsement from the master himself :

> *Nota:* En las opiniones que José Lezama Lima «me obliga a escribir con su pletórica pluma», hay ideas que reconozco como mías y otras que no. Pero lo que no reconozco como mío tiene una calidad que me obliga también a no abandonarlo como ajeno. Además el diálogo está en algunos momentos fundido, no es del uno ni del otro, sino del espacio y el tiempo medios.
>
> He preferido recoger todo lo que mi amigo me adjudica y hacerlo mío

en lo posible, a protestarlo con un no firme, como es necesario hacer a veces con el supuesto escrito ajeno de otros y fáciles dialogadores.[7]

Furthermore, Lezama's role as catalyst and axis of a remarkable group of Cuban artists organised around a shared cultural endeavour, turned him, only a few years after Juan Ramón's visit, into the driving force of *Orígenes,* which Juan Ramón regarded as one of the most worthwhile cultural publications in the Hispanic world of the 1940s and early 1950s, on both sides of the Atlantic, and to which he regularly contributed during its twelve years of activity between 1944 and 1956.[8] Finally, Cintio Vitier, the youngest of the three, has emerged as the principal chronicler of Juan Ramón's Cuban interlude. Apart from recording the impressionable memories of an adolescent faced with the imposing figure of the master, Vitier's critical coverage of the repercussions of Juan Ramón's visit extends to a thought-provoking exploration of its historical and political significance, especially in the context of the Cuban Revolution.

The three Cuban poets selected offer an interesting panorama of the different ways in which different poets assimilate to a different degree a shared formative experience. Florit, older and published before his personal encounter with the master, actually manifests the most derivative, least original, and least enriching assimilation. Lezama, the one whose hermetic poetry stands as most radically different from Juan Ramón's clear and accessible expression, actually engages the Spanish master in a sustained dialogue about poetics, widely recognised as one of Juan Ramón's most positive and forceful encounters with the valid intricacies and peculiarities of Latin American letters. The contact of Vitier with Juan Ramón allows us to see the awed response of the youngest of them all, as he recoils from the initial weight of the influence of the Jiménez present in Cuba, only to allow, years later, the last Juanramonian achievements of «Espacio» and *Animal de fondo* to make a marked impression on his work.

The correlation of what the three chosen Cuban poets might have shared with the master of novices during his visit will emphasise their common interests in poetry as a means of searching, finding, expressing, and making available experiences and interpretations of experience that revitalise spiritually —and even bodily— the individual poet, and by extension, the individual poetry reader.

Finally, I shall explore the different stances that all four poets de-

---

[7] Prefatory statement by Juan Ramón himself appended to Lezama's «Coloquio con Juan Ramón Jiménez», *Obras completas,* 3 vols. (México, 1977), II, p. 44. See also Vitier, ed., *Juan Ramón Jiménez en Cuba,* p. 155.

[8] «*Orígenes* me gusta *mucho* [JRJ's italics]. Estas revistas de ustedes me ilusionan más que las grandes y mezcladas. Dígale a Lezama que le estoy copiando una serie de aforismos y déle ese poema inédito y muchos recuerdos.» Carta a Cintio Vitier, 28 January 1946; *Cartas Literarias* (Barcelona, 1977), p. 160.

veloped after Juan Ramón's departure in January 1939, out of what they once shared: Juan Ramón's insistence on the ethical demands towards developing his «inmensa minoría», and his ego-theo-centric aesthetic mysticism; Florit's urban resignation, and subsequent static —almost defeatist— hope in conventional otherworldly redemption; Lezama's elaboration of his doctrines of always attempting the impossible and of the challenges of the Resurrection; and Vitier's both critical and committed involvement with the promises of the Cuban Revolution; all different ends of their once confluent and related poetic and spiritual pursuits.

Not losing complete sight of the excitement, the generosity, the receptivity, and all other intricacies of contact, love and tensions involved in the exchanges of *maestrías* and *aprendizajes,* we will necessarily depend, not on a reconstruction of their relationships, but rather on the traces of their dialogues still discernible in their *obras.*

I

SEEING, SAYING AND SALVAGING IN THE POETRY OF JUAN RAMON JIMENEZ

How much of Juan Ramón might have been known in Cuba when he arrived? The youngest hosts of the Spanish master corroborate what might have been inferred from a glance at the dates of Juan Ramón's publications. Fina García Marruz recalls:

> Cuando Juan Ramón vino a La Habana yo tenía trece años. (...) Con motivo de la visita de Juan Ramón, mi padre me regaló por las Navidades su gran libro dorado y blanco, *Canción,* exquisitamente impreso bajo la dirección del poeta, antes de la guerra.[1]

Cintio Vitier, in turn, remembers another book with an even more pronounced degree of veneration:

> Yo acababa de pasarme varios meses leyendo y releyendo el primer libro de poesía verdadera que había caído en mis manos. La *Segunda antolojía poética* de Juan Ramón, librito encuadernado en pasta azul que había encontrado en la biblioteca de mi padre, talismán que guardo contra todo mal. Tenía entonces quince años (...).[2]

Using those corroborations it can be argued that the poetry of *Diario de un poeta recién casado* (1916), *Eternidades* (1916-17), *Piedra y cielo* (1917-18), and all that came before, was well known, at least through the substantial selection of the *Segunda antolojía;* that the two releases of 1923 *Poesía* and *Belleza* were, at least, available; and that the poetry of *Canción* (1936) at that very juncture enjoyed the status of *novedad.* Of course, *Platero y yo* (1914) stood —*capítulo aparte*— as a revered classic and best seller.

It is very difficult to assess the availability of Juan Ramón's *cuader-*

---

[1] FINA GARCÍA MARRUZ interviewed by CIRO BIANCHI ROSS, in «El momento cubano de Juan Ramón Jiménez», *La Gaceta de Cuba,* no. 77 (October 1969), p. 8, col. 4.

[2] CINTIO VITIER interviewed in «El momento cubano de Juan Ramón Jiménez», p. 9, col. 2. For an even more lyrical account of Vitier's attachment to the *Segunda antolojía poética,* see his novelistic memoir *De Peña Pobre* (México, 1978), pp. 44-46.

nos and *hojas sueltas* published between 1923 and 1935, but the safest speculation, based mostly on their originally limited circulation, would lead us to infer that they were not readily available. The poetry of those ten to twelve years before the outbreak of the Civil War would finally appear in one book in 1946, under the title of *La estación total*.[3] However, a significant number of these poems were made public through magazine contributions. In Cuba, specifically, between 1937 and 1941, there were four major releases of this kind, three *entregas* under the title of «De mi 'Diario poético'»,[4] and another with the poems selected for his radio reading entitled «Ciego ante ciegos».[5] By 1936, *Canción* already included a large proportion of these previously unpublished poems dating from before the Civil War.

To concur with the widely accepted definition of Juan Ramón's second period as the one contained between his two trips to America (1916-1936), his poetic curriculum will be regarded as fully developed, formulated and exemplified in the poetry included between *Diario de un poeta recién casado* and *La estación total*. Then, considering the accessibility of this part of his work in Cuba by 1936, it can be safely inferred that his disciples were ready to receive him in person, after a good deal of exposure to his word in print.

The poetry of Juan Ramón before 1936 can be approached by asking the following questions: What do young poets learn from Juan Ramón? What did Juan Ramón mean to teach them, or anyone? Asking those questions brings to mind the forceful terms of one of Ezra Pound's letters: «It's all rubbish to pretend that art isn't didactic. A revelation is always didactic».[6]

Juan Ramón also uses forceful terms when he inaugurates, with *Eternidades* (1916-1917),[7] the most openly didactic part of his career.

[3] *Unidad* (1925), *Obra en marcha* (1928), *Sucesión* (1932), *Presente* (1933), and *Hojas* (1935), released in very carefully elaborated editions under the direct supervision of Juan Ramón have been re-issued ni one volume, *Cuadernos de Juan Ramón Jiménez*, Francisco Garfias, ed. (Madrid, 1960). See also bibliographical comments and notes in Antonio Sánchez Romeralo's introduction to Jiménez's *Leyenda* (Madrid, 1978), pp. ix-x.

[4] A) *Revista Cubana*, 7, nos. 19-21 (January-March 1937), pp. 55-57; this first set of «fragmentos» «De mi 'Diario poético'» (1936-37) is reprinted in *Juan Ramón Jiménez en Cuba*, pp. 35-51. B) *Universidad de la Habana*, no. 15 (November-December 1937), p. 5-17; the second set of «fragmentos» also appear reprinted in *Juan Ramón Jiménez en Cuba*, pp. 94-106. C) *Universidad de la Habana*, nos. 36-37 (May-August 1941), pp. 7-24; the third «entrega» (1937-39) is reprinted in *Juan Ramón Jiménez en Cuba*, pp. 119-32.

[5] *Revista Cubana*, 10, nos. 28-30 (October-December 1937), pp. 35-51; the transcript of the broadcast is reprinted in *Juan Ramón Jiménez en Cuba*, pp. 80-92.

[6] *The Letters of Ezra Pound* (London, 1950), p. 248. The letter goes on to say: «Only aesthetes since 1880 have pretended the contrary, and they aren't a very sturdy lot.»

[7] Howard T. Young in «The Exact Names», *MLN*, 96 (1981), p. 212, says the following about the opening pieces of *Eternidades* («Acción», «Inteligencia, dame»,

¡Intelijencia, dame
el nombre esacto de las cosas!
    Que mi palabra sea
la cosa misma,
creada por mi alma nuevamente.
Que por mí vayan todos
los que no las conocen, a las cosas;
que por mí vayan todos
los que ya las olvidan, a las cosas;
que por mí vayan todos
los mismos que las aman, a las cosas...
¡Intelijencia, dame
el nombre esacto, y tuyo,
y suyo, y mío, de las cosas![8]

The petition, pronounced through so many imperative verbs, sounds, in fact, imperious, and the reader has to determine whether the imperiousness expresses an urgent humility that needs to ask loudly for what it lacks, or an empowered faith that already envisages clearly what it will get. In either case, the owner of the voice can be recognised as someone who wants to become a priest, a teacher, or at least a facilitator of everybody's arrival at the full discovery of the relationship between words, meanings, and things.

This strong statement of desire and intent at the beginning of *Eternidades* follows a less haughty poem in which Howard T. Young recognises a state of «fluidity and apprenticeship»:[9]

No sé con qué decirlo
porque aún no está hecha
mi palabra.

(*LP*, p. 551)

Yet implicit in the adverb «aún» is the faith that, soon or sometime, his word will in fact be made, and his capacity to say it will in fact be actualised. The combination of this faith which determines the calling of a word-sayer, and of those uncertainties which issue from the present incapacity to say the words, redefines the state of «fluidity and apprenticeship» as the juncture at which the novice stands and says: «I know I will become a monk, a teacher, a poet, soon or sometime, but I don't really know what it all entails; show me.»

---

and «Vino, primera, pura»): «Their presence initiates a period in Juan Ramón's work in which, like Mallarmé and Valery, he will spend creative energy turning into poetry deliberations on the act of poetry.» See also Cole's *The Religious Instinct in the Poetry of Juan Ramón Jiménez* (Oxford, 1967), p. 55; and Mervyn Coke-Enguídanos's *Word and Work in the Poetry of Juan Ramón Jiménez* (London, 1982), pp. 44-47.

[8] *Libros de poesía*, Agustín Caballero, ed. (Madrid, 1967), p. 553. Quotations from this volume will hereafter be designated in parenthesis by the abbreviation *LP*.

[9] YOUNG, p. 212.

In the initial pieces of *Eternidades,* Juan Ramón voices his ambivalence about his state of knowing where he wants to go, not yet fully in possession of the means to get there. Nevertheless, already twenty years into his poetic practice, he could not help presenting, side by side with his ambivalence, solid evidence to demonstrate that he already knew a great deal about the demands and directions of his vocation.

Between «No sé con qué decirlo», and «¡Intelijencia, dame...!» there is a short poem which introduces the issue of «eternidades» as intimately related to a process of recreating the fullness experienced in our succession of intense moments in order to overcome the threats and losses imposed by the passage of time:

> Plenitud de hoy es
> ramita en flor de mañana.
> Mi alma ha de volver a hacer
> el mundo como mi alma.
>
> (*LP*, p. 552)

The fullness of the present moment is not only the state or condition from which all becoming gets even more intense; that fullness actually defines what the soul is in its most pronounced pitch of activity, and from the strength of a soul defined as such, the self extracts the energy to infuse the world with life, whenever it runs down, whenever it requires to be refilled or remade. The *modernista* imposition of an internal mood —usually nostalgia or depression— appears here as an impulse that energises and revitalises, asserting the primacy of the soul as the repository of essences that have to be discovered in order to define or remake the outside world in accord with them. That kind of «volver a ser» becomes one of Juan Ramón's most explicitly documented motions of the spirit; and this study intends to center its discussion of what the master might have shared with or passed on to his apprentices precisely around these concerns.

The way in which poetry is central to the processes involved in «volver a hacer» is already evident as early as *Diario de un poeta recién casado* (1916), even if Jiménez is not yet writing poetry specifically about poetry.

> Te tenía olvidado,
> cielo, y no eras
> más que un vago esistir de luz,
> visto —sin nombre—
> por mis cansados ojos indolentes.
> Y aparecías, entre las palabras
> perezosas y desesperanzadas del viajero,
> como en breves lagunas repetidas
> de un paisaje de agua visto en sueños...

22

Hoy te he mirado lentamente,
y te has ido elevando hasta tu nombre.

(*LP*, p. 262)

The opening statement in the poem, establishes the *Yo* as the subject of the action, and the same *Yo* also acts as the subject in the first independent clause of the last sentence. Between the initial admission of forgetfulness, and the final motion of careful attention that reestablishes the contact between «palabra-nombre» and «la cosa misma», the poem does use the sky as a subject, but emphasizing how the tiredness and indolence of the eyes, and the slothful and despairing words of the traveller, misrepresent the reality of the given. At first and always, «cielo» is fully «cielo», and there is a word «cielo» for it which fully names it; what is given at the beginning of the poem, however, amounts to a confession of forgetfulness of the forever available coincidence of name and thing. Even if the «cielo» does achieve the unqualified status of active subject in the final clause of the poem, the achievement documented in the poem as a whole is not primarily the ascension of this «cielo» to the heights where it meets its name. In line with the confessional tone of the first stanza which deals exclusively with the consequences and the pains of having forgotten, the final sentence ascribes the redemptive opening to that attentive, grace-filled displacement or re-placement of the gaze of the poet upwards, towards the thing itself. The poet's «mirar» does more than accompany or aid the ascension; the lifting of his gaze, his *sursum corda,* the central drama of the poem, is precisely what fills the scenario of this rediscovery of «cielo», in space as well as in the grid of well-tuned names, and makes the miracle happen.[10]

Establishing or reestablishing the connection between word, name, meaning and thing, by bringing ourselves to attention, those connections —the contents of the revelation— can be expressed by virtue of the apprehended adequacy of the words to name the things. For Juan Ramón poetry is the process of setting all that down, making it available as a catalyst or map or primer or mirror for future redemptive episodes.[11]

---

[10] This interpretation of «Cielo» was elaborated taking issue with that of Mervyn Coke-Enguídanos as it appeared in «Word and Work (with capital letters) in Juan Ramón Jiménez», *MLN,* 96 (1981), pp. 226-27. I objected that her basically adequate account detracted from the full and proper appreciation of the role of the individual within the redemptive episode. I was happy to find, however, that the discussion of this poem in her book-length study *Work and Work in the Poetry of Juan Ramón Jiménez* (London, 1982), pp. 67-70, answers my objections, as it recasts the terms of her original presentation in ways that are substantially more engaging.

[11] As late as December 1953 JUAN RAMÓN would say to RICARDO GULLÓN: «Para mí corregir es revivir; revivo momentos de mi vida cuando corrijo los poemas escritos en el pasado, y espero que otras personas cuando los lean, sentirán impresiones análogas a las que yo siento.» *Conversaciones con Juan Ramón Jiménez* (Ma-

Any record of how paying attention buys revelations is in itself a call to attention, an opening to opportunities in which «Mi alma ha de volver —a Ser— a hacer el mundo».

These calls to attention, these repeated rekindlings of the capacity to revitalise the world, can be characterised by the suggestiveness of a resonant etymological play. Juan Ramón's deepest didactic impetus can be defined as a crusade to *suscitate*[12] *again and again* the fullness of life in moments of plenitude. Juan Ramón, like his «mirlo fiel», «ensancha con su canto la hora parada de la estación viva, y nos hace la vida suficiente» (*LP*, p. 1262). For these *resuscitations,* Juan Ramón catches these moments in his loyal net of words,[13] keeps them alive in his *Obra,* and provides, through the possibility of re-creative readings, an access to revitalizing revelations.

This presentation could continue with a detailed discussion of Juan Ramón's trajectory, from his condition as a man beset by all the traditional and contemporary threats of Death and Nothingness, through his aesthetic affirmation of Beauty in the practice of poetry, and all the way to the mystical arrival at the discovery of his very own «dios deseado y deseante». However, given that the bibliography of Juanramoniana already includes a substantial number of successful attempts to document such a trajectory, and specific parts thereof, it seems more productive to refer to their observations as they become pertinent to this pursuit of what the Master and the younger Cuban poets might have shared.

For now, suffice it to acknowledge that Juan Ramón's desire to become a leader in the cultivation of habits of seeing and saying and saving sometimes reaches extremes from which he dares to proclaim his own elevation to the post of Master of Eternities. *Eternidades* (1916-17) ends with the following loud assurance of his capacity to fulfil his vocation, in terms of the adequacy of his word to survive as disembodied essences after his body's death:

> ¡Palabra mía eterna!
> ¡Oh, qué vivir supremo
> —ya en la nada la lengua de mi boca—,
> oh, qué vivir divino
> de flor sin tallo y sin raíz,

---

drid, 1958), pp. 119-20. See also the discussion of «corregir es revivir» in Coke-Enguídanos's book, p. 62.

[12] Even if now rare, the verb «to suscitate» is listed in the *Oxford English Dictionary* as having been used with the following meanings: *a)* to stir up, to excite; *b)* to raise (a person) out of inactivity, to exalt the condition of; *c)* to impart life or activity, to quicken, vivify, animate.

[13] What JORGE GUILLÉN refered to as «la fiel plenitud de las palabras».

nutrida, por la luz, con mi memoria,
sola y fresca en el aire de la vida!

(*LP*, p. 688)

No matter how difficult it is to accept the ultimate validity of Juan Ramón's hypertrophied sense of self-importance, we have to bow to the way in which he incarnates Cortázar's caustic definition of genius: «el genio es elegirse y *acertar*.»[14] Juan Ramón chose to be what he in fact became. Every time he makes a revelation accessible, his poems stand as records of his secular resuscitations and as means for our own; his poetry as a whole becomes a summa of the processes involved in the business of revitalizing existence, and his practice of writing poetry achieves the status of a sustained vocation in the habits of resurrection.

Any modern Dante would find Juan Ramón among the envious in Purgatory, or among the sowers of discord in Hell,[15] but once again the apprentice would have to bend his gaze down to this new Ser Brunetto and acknowledge:

m'insegnavate come l'uom s'etterna.[16]

---

[14] *Rayuela* (Buenos Aires, 1968), p. 463.
[15] NERUDA, for instance, cannot refrain from ascribing to Juan Ramón both envy and an acute aptitude for discord, at the same time that he acknowledges the validity of Juan Ramón's *obra*: «Juan Ramón Jiménez, poeta de gran esplendor, fue el encargado de hacerme conocer la legendaria envidia española. Este gran poeta que no necesitaba envidiar a nadie, puesto que su obra es un gran resplandor que comienza con la oscuridad del siglo, vivía como un falso ermitaño, zahiriendo desde su escondite a cuanto creía que le hacía sombra». *Confieso que he vivido* (Barcelona, 1974), p. 167.
[16] «(...) you taught me how man makes himself eternal.» *Inferno*, XV, 85.

II

JUAN RAMON IN PUERTO RICO (1936): «MANO AMIGA»

Juan Ramón himself makes a vivid *estampa* out of his most sentimentally charged encounter with one young poetry writer in the Caribbean. The *estampa* first appeared under the title of «Mano amiga, 'El poetastro' (Río Piedras)»:[1]

> En la honda sombra triangular de la puertecilla, (...) el «poetastro», como un animal alegre y fuerte, me buscaba tímidamente la mano.
>
> Su mano era corta, maciza, como cortada a la medida de su estrecha frente de surcos, en la que el pelo nacía en punta extraña, como en una nuca. Toda su mole de 15 años, su ser de carne chata, cuyo resorte parecía residir en su nariz en conato, estaba vuelto y trastornado, equivocado, confuso. Cuando, después de una esterna salida irónica, su boca se reía encogiendo en su frunce toda su vida, la nueva cara de todo aquello daba idea de otra posibilidad humana.
>
> Yo lo miraba con respeto angustioso. (...) Parecía lleno de confianza en su secreto. Declamó con acción y adorno:
>
> > ... tu voz suena feliz en mi oído,
> > como el soplo encantador de Eolo
> > cuando, ya el Astro mirífico dormido,
> > va por las palmeras con ardiente dolo;
> > dulce Maestra...
>
> Cada vez que se refería en verso o prosa a la voz dulce de su maestra, su cara se transformaba, temblando de manera terrible. Como que saliera de un subterráneo a la luz del sol más divino, en una resurrección espantosa de lo muerto. Era feroz su expresión, la de un criminal contra el destino, contra sí mismo o contra dios.
>
> No dudaba, reía seguro, dueño de todo lo que no veía. Siguió:
>
> > ... dulce Maestra,
> > no me abandones solo en un sentido,
> > pues no me falta más que uno solo...

[1] «De mi 'Diario práctico' 1937-39 (Fragmento)», *Universidad de la Habana* nos. 36-37 (May-August 1941), pp. 12-14. Also reprinted in *Isla de la simpatía*, pp. 65-67, but under the unfortunately shorter title of «'El poetastro' (Río Piedras)».

Al terminar, después de un momento de vacilante acomodación, como si se quedara en un sitio que no era el suyo o decidiera por entonces quedarse con nosotros, se insultaba, se llamaba «incauto, bucólico, poetastro», siempre con su extrema risa antidiluviana.

Volvió a sentarse en su silla tieso, las manos cuadradas sobre los muslos, elevada la cara a no sé qué claro resplandeciente que le daba verdadera luz. Le hablé entonces sumiso, como a un superior distinto, de su poema. Le dije que los dos versos finales eran de gran poeta y que un hombre, un ser que expresaba su sentimiento como él, debía considerarse feliz.

It would have been enough to appreciate the lines quoted as an urgent plea from a boy who needs to thank his *maestra* for her efforts, to teach her a lesson about the validity of her practice of looking beyond his handicaps to his full humanity; but Juan Ramón does more than that. He casts himself within the parable as listener, critic, learner, and teacher. Furthermore, he casts the «poetastro» as a pathetic specimen of mangled humanity who commands «anguished respect» achieving dignity and freedom through the efficacy of a few lines of poetry that remake and preserve fully alive, the salutary presence of a teacher.

Once more, Juan Ramón identifies and validates the poetic action of rooting our capacity for resurrection in our capacity to voice and salvage. In this instance, his perception and appraisal of that saving poetic attitude appears acutely framed within the pathetic extremes of the external ugliness and imperfections of both the boy and the poem, and within the adequacy of the self-imposed derogatory name of «poetastro».

The «poetastro» also becomes for Juan Ramón someone to keep alive, someone with whom he once shared the surprise of catching himself learning and teaching in the same encounter. Part of the title, «Mano amiga», already bespeaks Juan Ramón's generous acknowledgement of a relatedness based on a poetic affinity more vitally unitive than any given or acquired peerage of accomplished craftsmen. The relatedness of those «manos amigas» is further documented in this piece by the circular referentiality of its objects and subjects. The piece amounts to a confession of the master poet that he has found himself *in statu pupillari*, before one of his least gifted novices, as the bad poetry of the boy eternalises the memory of yet another teacher. The boy's assertion of his dignity despite his external limitations teaches both teachers not to be blind to his worth, as he derives much of this worth from his faith in the teacher as a witness to what he really is.

The parable also demonstrates the extent to which Juan Ramón's contact with the young poets of the Caribbean is ultimately a matter of confluence, rather than influence. He arrives to find young poets writing; he decides to make himself available for comment; and in his exchanges he tries to point out those best efforts that could be most productively pursued. His guidance was not blatantly prescriptive or proscriptive, but rather, selective and encouraging. He allowed himself to label the best, the better, the good, or the not so good, without going to the Poundian extreme of «take this out», and «leave that in». The effluence of Juan Ramón's work and presence, and the receptivity of the novices graced by his visitations, endow him with the efficacy of a chosen exemplary poet who reads, listens, identifies, criticises, appraises, validates, and, most of all, endorses the many different ways and wills to continue writing.

After leaving Spain, and after the frustrating failure of his diplomatic mission to gain support in the United States for the Republican cause, Juan Ramón spent two very productive months in Puerto Rico. His anthology *Verso y prosa para niños* (1936) made available for Puerto Rican children a selection of his works similar to the one compiled by Zenobia and published in Spain for the same purpose in 1932. He started delivering public lectures, and he catalyzed the foundation of the «Fiesta por la Poesía y el Niño de Puerto Rico», and the preparation of an anthology of the poetry of the best young poets.

Perhaps Juan Ramón's gifts to Puerto Rico found the best recipient in the fifteen-year-old «poetastro» from Río Piedras, almost a child, almost a poet.

III

EUGENIO FLORIT AND THE MASTER:
THE WEIGHT OF AN INFLUENCE

Before discussing the nature of the *confluencia*, up to the point of
Juan Ramón's departure from Cuba in 1939, it must be acknowledged
that many other poets also practice their vocation in ways similar to
those so far ascribed to Juan Ramón: also grounding their expresion
of regenerative experience in that disciplined way of seeing attentively,
and of voicing their visions in tune with the adequacy of the words
to name the things, thus perpetuating the intensity of the moment.[1]
Since it can be said that so many poets work by virtue of their own way
of harnessing these habits, it may be inaccurate to claim that Juan Ramón was the one who taught any of it to anybody. But we will proceed
assured by the way in which the Cuban poets Juan Ramón met during
the late 1930s insist that they did learn much from him.

In November of 1936, Juan Ramón Jiménez arrives in Cuba. Vitier was
fifteen, Lezama almost twenty-six, the latter was on the brink of publishing his first poem, the former had not written more than a couple.

Florit was thirty-three, and had published his first two books of
poetry, which had already come to the attention of Juan Ramón in Spain.
In the following excerpt from Juan Ramón's prologue to Florit's *Doble
acento* (1930-1936), published in 1937, we can find Juan Ramón's most
significant endorsement of the poetic vocation of a younger American:

---

[1] «In an essay on the poetry of Jorge Guillén, Amado Alonso has observed that
a particular mark of poets since Mallarmé has been the intensity of their concern
to save what is lasting and essential from the certain wreckage of temporal existence [*Materia y forma en poesía*], and he adds that modern phenomenology has
defined this concern and examined it in reference to all sciences of the mind,
with the result that it can be seen as fundamental, not only in the creation of
poetry, but in the genesis of language itself. For language as a logical act of
exposition and differentiation by means of which the mind imposes upon the em-
pirical truth of Heraclitus's *panta rhei* the Eleatic concept of static simultaneity,
purely imaginary —that is, non-empirical— though it may be.» PAUL OLSON, *Circle
of Paradox: Time and Essence in the Poetry of Juan Ramón Jiménez* (Baltimore,
1967), p. 3.

Días después de llegar [a La Habana] oí en un acto público «El Martirio de San Sebastián» (...)

Me quedé contento. Hablé con Florit de su «San Sebastián» y pronto conocí otros nuevos poemas suyos de diferente sentido y otra perfección, poemas justos y poemas arbitrarios, en el centro de los cuales se me quedaba inalterable, con su claro movimiento natural resuelto en fe de estatua de la plaza de la belleza, con su afirmación sin réplica, aquel centro de una poesía juvenil. Y cuando repasé todo el libro *Doble acento,* le rogué a Florit que dejara en medio de las partes (dos caminos, uno al presente y otro al futuro), como centro, como alzado acento central, el *Martirio.*

La mirada en el libro, caía fija mi atención sobre los poemas que se levantaban, señal inequívoca de calidad, de su hoja. Pronto se levantó frente al «San Sebastián» una «Estatua», y me erguía su esbeltez en la tarde cubana de domingo tranquilo, desde una planta universal. (...) Los dos poemas, las dos figuras, Adán y Eva finales, el mártir de sangre, que se convierte en feliz símbolo plástico, y el símbolo plástico que se hace corriente sonrisa feliz, expresaron bien, a mi juicio, desde el primer día, los mejores misterios, los que yo querría ver seguidos, del arte poético de Eugenio Florit.[2]

Juan Ramón openly acknowledges that his advice originates from his own appreciation of the double emphasis, the two roads that he would like to see further pursued. It must be recognized that Florit himself had already defined this duality in a essay published in 1935:[3]

En mis poemas veréis cosas fijas, claras, de mármol —lo clásico en fin. Y otras desorbitadas, sin medida, oscuras. En unas, Goethe o Garcilaso —en otras Walt Whitman o Alberti. Pero en unas y otras estoy yo. (...)

El mismo título de mi libro futuro, «Doble acento» anuncia la dualidad a que antes aludí.

Although Juan Ramón's comments do not point to any new insights, they remain encouraging as a corroboration of the adequacy of the young poet's evaluation of his own paths of development.

Juan Ramón was clearly important to Florit even before his visit to Cuba. His name figures prominently in the lists of mentors volunteered by Florit as early as 1935. At the age of fifteen, he wrote his very first poems as he was reading «Baudelaire, Juan Ramón Jiménez, Martí, Rubén Darío y ¡ay! Francisco Villaespesa»; later he places his first collection of published juvenilia under the aegis of Hugo, Martí, Juan Ramón

---

[2] Juan Ramón's prologue also appeared as «El único estilo de Eugenio Florit», in *Revista Cubana,* 8, nos. 22-24 (April-June 1937). The quotation here is from yet another reprinting in *La corriente infinita,* Francisco Garfias, ed. (Madrid, 1961), pp. 143-46. See also *Juan Ramón Jiménez en Cuba,* pp. 52-65.

[3] «Una hora conmigo», *Revista Cubana,* 2, nos. 4-6 (1935), pp. 164-65. José OLIVIO JIMÉNEZ in his introduction to Florit's *Antología penúltima* (Madrid, 1970), pp. 17-20, also notes the echoes of Florits' own appraisal of the «doble acento», in anticipation of Juan Ramón's, and in line with both ends of the traditionally debated polarization of Spanish poetry based on Dámaso Alonso's «Escila y Caribdis...» of 1927: «poesía pura vs. superrealismo», or in Juan Ramón's own terms, «poemas justos vs. arbitrarios», «poesía neta vs. barroca».

Jiménez, and Amado Nervo; later still the *vanguardistas* and Góngora make their obligatory appearance in the lists.[4]

Though this discussion concentrates on what has been characterized as confluences, in the case of Florit it is necessary to explore the already widely recognized influence of Juan Ramón Jiménez.[5] Vitier himself attests to the development of this influence:

> Si por influencia entendemos algo que se refleja visiblemente en la escritura, creo que un solo poeta cubano recibió la impronta juanramoniana de ese modo. Me refiero a Eugenio Florit, cuyo granado *Doble acento* apareció con un prólogo fijador, traspasador de Juan Ramón. Florit fue cogido por el hechizo de la lucidez juanramoniana (no era para menos, es fácil hablar cuando no se ha *recibido* ese prólogo irresistible) de tal modo que su escritura posterior cambió en homenaje al prologuista, escogiendo de las dos líneas señaladas en su poesía, la «neta» frente a la «barroca», cuando en verdad Juan Ramón prefería la *fusión* de ambas líneas en «un solo estilo igual o encadenado», el rico contrapunto del «Martirio de San Sebastián» y las «Estrofas a una estatua». Bien, de una u otra forma, Juan Ramón estaba en su destino y Florit se juanramonizó hacia lo que prefería de sí mismo.[6]

As the information on Vitier and Lezama is presented, it will be necessary to reconsider the contrast between the substantial echoes of the master's voice within the poetry of the senior novice, and the less derivative, more individually incorporated traces in the work of the two younger poets.

«Interior», one of Florit's first poems, published before 1930, can be regarded as a good indicator of the terms in which he defined his vocation:

> Más hacia adentro, repliégate hacia ti
> —vida real mía.
> Reflejo, introspección.
> Cada vez más tuyo
> libertado de lazos exteriores
> —verso, vida real.
> Hacia adentro, hacia ti, lejos de fuera,
> sé rebelde en secreto,
> pero no llores.
> En ti no hallarás llanto.
> Cada vez más en ti, serás sereno,
> tu luz vertida en el espejo limpio
> —claro interior, luz clara.
> Concentrado en ti mismo serás el verso puro
> —etéreo, único, solo.

---

[4] «Una hora conmigo», pp. 159-64.

[5] See JOSÉ OLIVIO JIMÉNEZ, «La poesía de Eugenio Florit», *Antología penúltima* (Madrid, 1970), p. 21. Quotation of Florit's poetry appearing in this volume will be cited parenthetically with the abbreviation *AP*.

[6] «El momento cubano de Juan Ramón Jiménez», p. 9, col. 3-4.

No serás más que tú. Sólo tú. Sólo luz.
Y sin el lastre secular estarás áureo,
libre ya, libertado de la tierra.[7]

This can be shown to be uncannily confluent with the terms in which Juan Ramón defined his spiritual ambitions during his second period: the plea for a fuller self-surrender to introspection and vital searches; that pursuit of freedom from external necessity; the equation of personal identity, true life and poetry; the eagerness to essentialize, turning all experience into light and clarity; and the acts of poetry to formulate and actualize his pleas, pursuits, equations and ambitions, are all concerns of the poetics of Juan Ramón Jiménez, especially in *Eternidades*, *Piedra y Cielo*, *Poesía*, *Belleza* and *La estación total*.

It is highly unlikely that Florit could have read the following poem by Juan Ramón Jiménez before writing «Interior». It first appeared in the extremely limited edition of *Hojas* (1933), and then as the first piece in «La estación total» (1923-1936) which was not published until the Argentine edition of 1946:

Rompió mi alma con oro.
Y como májica palmera
reclinada en su luz,
me acarició, mirándome
desde dentro, los ojos.

Me dijo con su iris:
«Seré la plenitud
de tus horas medianas.
Subiré con hervor tu hastío,
daré a tu duda espuma.»

Desde entonces ¡qué paz!
no tiendo ya hacia afuera
mis manos. Lo infinito
está dentro. Yo soy
el horizonte recojido.

Ella, Poesía, Amor, el centro
indudable.

(*LP*, p. 1135)

Nonetheless, the same motifs used to develop the same concerns yield two strictly related poems, voiced from two very different perspectives: the mature poet, in fact, broadcasts the certainty of possessing what the neophyte asks for.

Even at this early stage in his career Florit has charted his faith; he has voiced his desires through the urgent introspective imperatives, «repliégate hacia ti», «sé rebelde en secreto»; and he has voiced his faithful

---

[7] *Poema mío* (México, 1947), p. 55; hereafter cited parenthetically.

expectations of ontological fullness through the indicative futurity of «no hallarás el llanto», «serás sereno», «serás el verso puro», «No serás más que tú», «estarás áureo, libre ya». Face to face, the subject of «Interior» had to recognize in the subject of «Desde dentro» an accomplished guide, who already possessed the peace of being fully satisfied in that self-contained completeness which thrives on the active relationships of his «alma» with three identified centres of existence: «Ella. Poesía. Amor.»

That internal expanse occupied by the self becomes for Juan Ramón and Florit —as well as for Lezama, Vitier, and so many other poets, ontologists and epistomologists— the principal object of their knowing, the stage of experience, searches and discoveries. In fact, elements of the external world will be experienced, searched for, and attentively discovered and rediscovered insofar as they are made to penetrate that volume encompassed by the self. We have already seen Juan Ramón expanding the radius of his vital sphere to include the proper perception of «Cielo»; and this expansion remains centred on the core of the poetic-self where the concordance of things and names takes place. These motions of centering and expanding the self are clearly elaborated in the following poem from *Poesía* (1917-1923) as a self-imposed imperative to grow towards a distant selfhood that is both ego-centric, and completely immersed in the fullness of reality—«todo»:

¡Concentrarme, concentrarme,
hasta oírme el centro último,
el centro que va a mi yo
más lejano,
el que me sume en el todo!

(*LP*, p. 898)

Florit's urgency to look inward, already evident as early as «Interior», swells to the high pitch of the visceral imagery in «Canción Pequeñita», one of the earliest poems of *Doble acento* (1930-1936); in which the reference to the master is explicitly acknowledged by using two lines by Juan Ramón as the epigramatic point of departure:

¡Aquí está! ¡Venid todos!
¡Cavad! ¡Cavad! ¡Cavad!

J.R.J.

Para alimento de peces y de aves,
para el cerdo y el pico del buitre,
aquí está, medroso, con la inquietud del ciervo perseguido.
No importa. Buscadlo. ¡Cavad!

Si tenéis que encontrarlo por el recuerdo del latido
y el recuerdo del clavel y de la llama.
Es tan tímido que muere a cada suspiro sin aliento,
para reír después, de un barco de papel puesto en el agua.

33

Venid, digo. Cavad hasta encontrar a ese cobarde
temblando y rojo de vergüenza.
¡Cavad! Lo encontraréis hecho de muerte.
Entonces, arrojadlo lejos de mí, a los vientos,
como una amapola despedazada.

(Poema mío, p. 122)

The speaker digs into his own flesh to find, to know, and to extirpate, a lack of courage in the heart, not only the most vulnerable part of the self, but the very seat of fear and mortality: «cobarde (...) hecho de muerte.» The search for all this negativity depends on following the scent of memories of the living «latido», and the fragile beauty and efficacy of «clavel» and «llama», memories which inhabit the same organ together with the fear and the mortality. The dénouement of the spiritual experience achieves a highly positive resolution of the Christian command to «cut off» those members accountable for sinning (Matthew 5:29-30, Mark 9:43). This patently sacrificial, retributive cleasing takes the organ, the seat of the sickness unto death, casts it off; not down and away as detritus, but up, to the wind, where its *despedazamiento* has less to do with decay than with the explosive, saving expansion —*sursum corda*— of the self beyond those limitations accounted for in the act of internal revelation.

Florit crafted his compelling gloss on the Juanramonian imperative in his least Juanramonian voice —loose metrics, surreal imagery. The relative impurity of this poem could be seen as representative of the «arbitrary» or «baroque» *acento* which Juan Ramón had recognized as an important facet of Florit's poetry. Despite their stylistic dissimilarities, however «Canción pequeñita» still keeps a high level of consonance with the thematic thrust of the poem it refers to, «Perro divino», from *Piedra y Cielo* (1917-1918):

¡Aquí está! ¡Venid todos!
¡Cavad, cavad!

¡Mis manos echan sangre
y ya no pueden más!

Aquí está.

¡Entre la tierra húmeda,
qué olor, a eternidad!

Aquí está.

¡Oíd mi aullido largo
contra el sol inmortal!

¡Aquí está! ¡Venid todos!
¡Cavad, cavad, cavad!

(LP, p. 749)

34

The same imperative to seek manifests its urgency in the bleeding hands of the digger, in the exalted exclamatory assertion of the proximity of the treasure searched for, and in the canine envy of the sun's possession of the coveted hidden thing. Juan Ramón's poem formulates the need and will to persevere in the pursuit of that eternity or immortality already beleaguered —hounded— by the seeker's efforts, while Florit stresses the excess of fear and mortality against which he has to exert his need and will to make himself less limited, less mortal.

The internal upheavals so adequately manifested in Florit's impure poetry tend to subside as he gravitates more and more towards that realm of his poetic expression most thoroughly akin to Juan Ramón's manner of voicing even internal upheaval in limpid and measured registers. All critics of Florit's poetry identify in his pursuit of serenity and harmony the central task of his poetic development during the 30s and 40s.[8] Florit achieves in his *Reino* (1938) that serenity already envisioned before 1930 in the «serás sereno» of «Interior». But despite having achieved a type of poetry most consonant with the master's voice, attesting to a spiritual state quite actively aspired to by the master himself, the serene completeness of *Reino* appears divorced from Florit's more turbulent motions, failing to manifest those ambitious guidelines Juan Ramón prescribed for growing seekers: the doctrine of *éstasis dinámico*.

The following two poems by Florit appear in *Reino* under the blatantly Juanramonian rubric of «Canciones»:

3

Al agua la piedra, al agua la hoja,
al agua clara del remanso.

Al agua la estrella, al agua la luna,
al agua clara del remanso.

Al agua tu risa, al agua tu rostro,
al agua clara del remanso.

Al agua mi pena, al agua mi sueño,
al agua clara del remanso.

4

Cuando sea la tierra mi pan y mi vino
habré encontrado el sueño para siempre.
Todo un sueño de siglos, de primaveras y de inviernos
que pasarán sobre mis huesos fríos.

---

[8] *«Asonante final» y otros poemas (1946-1955)* (La Habana, 1956), and his subsequent poetry return to a voice that is less Juanramonian due to its conversational and confessional tenor; this will be discussed further on as part of the exploration of the four poets' divergences.

Y así estará mi jugo de poeta
vertiéndose en regatos interiores
para salir al sol en aguas cristalinas.

(*Antología penúltima*, pp. 128-9)

Now let us look at a third poem, from Juan Ramón's *Poesía* of 1923, entitled «En lo oscuro» in *Canción*, and «Anochecer (Brisa y agua)» in the *Tercera Antolojía Poética* and *Libros de poesía*.

Riillos tenues, puros
en lo oscuro corren
—red plata en lo azul—,
trayéndome flores...

—Ay, el agua eterna,
por la tierra negra;
la infinita brisa,
por la sombra fría!—

... Trayéndome estrellas;
y estoy en lo oscuro,
como un árbol lúgubre
nutridos de mundos.

(*LP*, p. 924)

Juan Ramón places the blackness and darkness of earth and night side by side with the fertility and brightness promised by the rivulets that bring flowers and stars. The achieved revelation includes both positive and negative elements, and the negative elements appear not merely as what needs to be overcome, but as the very source of positivity and possibility. Florit's «canciones» using almost the same elemental vocabulary, and similarly structured verse forms, uphold the primacy of an achieved stasis. This might bring to mind Juan Ramón's exploration of his ambition for peace, but he would have found such stasis too limiting, as he would always concern himself more with the spiritual and poetic processes involved in the struggle towards peace, than with peace itself. Every element in Florit's first song is reduced to the same status, «Al agua»; every member of the catalogue is either thrown in, reflected from, or cleansed by the tranquility of the waters, the calmness of which drowns the need to struggle towards the desired serenity. The poem still works as a peace-giving artefact, but it cannot be regarded as an imperative to hold the negative and the positive, the challenging and the peace giving, the unknown and discovered in ever-developing and uplifting vital tension.[9]

---

[9] OLSON, p. 13, asserts the following about Juan Ramón's guardedness towards «pure stasis»: «Certainly the antivital implications of pure stasis were evident to Juan Ramón, and he constantly sought to retain within the static moment the

The second of Florit's «canciones» falls short of Juan Ramón's pursuits and aspirations even more pronouncedly than the previous one. The latter song takes the stasis to buried *Reinos,* where the hope of a resurgence sustains the internal poetic effluences, but it keeps it inactive, unmanifested until the expected point of resurrection. Juan Ramón would have scorned the modest lack of impetus of this «jugo de poeta» —so willing to remain contained— with his taunting expression of the eminently active fate of his words after his disappearance, the already quoted «¡Palabra mía eterna! / ¡Oh, qué vivir supremo / —ya en la nada la lengua de mi boca— (...)!» (*LP,* p. 688).

So far we have seen Florit's poetry of the late 30s affected by his contact with Juan Ramón in ways that would have left the master at least partially dissatisfied. There is a letter from Juan Ramón to Florit in which the praise openly given could be reinterpreted as Juan Ramón's subtextual expression of his dissatisfaction:

> Mi querido Eugenio Florit:
>
> estos poemas últimos de usted (las «Canciones» y el «Preludio») creo que señalan el oasis adonde han salido los dos bellos caminos que usted traía (neoclasicismo y sobrerealismo conciente). (...)
> Para mí, ha encontrado usted su «Reino» (un buen título para su libro venidero). (...)
>
> La Habana, julio, 1937.[10]

More than implicitly, the master's evaluation equates *reino* with *oasis,* and this equation belittles, not only the nature of the *Reino,* but the ultimate worth of a quest for sovereignty over such a limited and marginal space. If Florit finds or makes his peace and his salvation in a paradise as far removed from reality and as circumscribed as an oasis tends to be, then he has not followed Juan Ramón's curriculum for remaking the world very convincingly. Leo R. Cole aptly describes the nature and extent of Juan Ramón's *reino* as much more inclusive:

> The possibility that there might be, in the process of cultivating the other immortal self which is intuitively perceived, a chance of salvation from death leads the poet to construct, on a conceptual level at least, a magnificent edifice of ideas around his spiritual «yo». (...) This position is reached in *La estación total* (1923-1936), a book in which the self-sufficiency of the world created by Juan Ramón is most easily identified with the self-sufficiency of the poet's essential self.[11]

---

kinetic qualities of life itself. The ideal, as he expressed it in an aphorism of his *Etica estética,* was 'An ecstasis which does not kill what is alive'.»

[10] *Cartas literarias* (Barcelona, 1977), p. 20. This letter was first published in «De mi 'Diario poético' 1937-39 (fragmento)», *Universidad de la Habana,* nos. 36-37 (May-August 1941), pp. 19-20.

[11] COLE, pp. 61-62.

By 1936 Juan Ramón had not yet achieved his mystical arrival at the vision of *Dios deseado y deseante,* but so far his trajectory had taken him through the intermediate stages of creating through his poetry «a kind of world of its own (...) fit for a God to inhabit».[12] In his poem «En lo oscuro» we have already witnessed his spirit rooted in potentiality and negativity, feeding on whole worlds, «como un árbol lúgubre nutrido de mundos». An *oasis* could have never contained his *reino.*

Leaving aside for a moment the differences, let us return to the documentation of the «confluencia» of the master and his eldest, most influenced novice. Let us create an interstice where the nature of their dialogue can be manifest: to the left, Florit's 1935 appraisal of the implications of his vocation,[13] to the right, that part of Juan Ramón's poetic doctrine most clearly applicable to the poetry of *Doble acento* (1937):[14]

Toda una serie de imágenes se da cita en alguna circunvolución cerebral para producir lo que llamamos «hecho poético puro». Este hecho poético es en su esencia un estado de pensamiento, totalmente distinto de los estados del alma que se traducían, en otro tiempo, en el derrame, por todos los poros del yo-sentimiento, de un sudor lírico, en la acepción peyorativa del vocablo. La razón poética ya, afortunadamente, se ha desligado de la razón lógica. Para el poeta existe una verdad. *Su* verdad, que no corresponde con la verdad del matemático, del basurero, de la señora de su casa. El hecho de que esa verdad suya sea distinta de la de los demás constituye su tragedia y, también, su gloria. Además, es su pecado. El pecado de *poetizar,* en lugar de *ser,* como expresa Kierkegaard. Pero es que el poeta, mientras poetiza, ¿no está *siendo*? ¿Es que para *ser* es preciso no poetizar? El hombre en trance de poesía vive un mundo suyo, con una perfecta organización, suya también, y una filosofía propia. Y en él *es* como su verdad le obliga a ser. Con todas las implicaciones que se derivan de estar viviendo su verdad.

Y el verso no es más denso por contener palabras más pesadas, plomo, adoquín, etc., sino por contener lo alto y lo profundo. El éstasis pesa más que el movimiento. El verdadero dinamismo es éstasis, fuerza hacia dentro, hacia el centro, fuerza que no se pierde, fuerza que nos da enerjía bella fundamental. Acto de poderío inmanente, en que nuestro ser llega, por intensidad de contemplación, a darse cuenta de su elemento, a entenderse, como otro elemento, con los elementos, el agua que se busca, el aire inseparable, el fuego totalizador, la entrañable tierra; en que nuestro ser encuentra por su vida su secreto, su destino, su eternidad. Este es el «estado poético», lírico, de que ya no volvemos nunca aunque volvamos a lo otro, la consecución suma, y que puede ser en nosotros tan natural como el sueño, siempre lijero por pesado que sea. Y dichoso aquel, Eugenio Florit, en quien la poesía es, despierto, tan corriente, tan fácil, tan graciosa, tan usual, tan diaria en su sorpresa como el sueño al dormido. Sueño y poesía nos hacen existir con el cuerpo como gracia continente, para el alma como gloria contenida.

---

[12] COLE, p. 46.
[13] «Una hora conmigo», p. 166.
[14] *La corriente infinita,* p. 148.

Both poets place the acts of poetry at the core of their processes of self-definition. Florit's programme, centered on the adoption of a discovered, formulated, and binding truth, which organizes reality making him answerable to the covenant with his own truth, is perfectly consonant with Juan Ramón's curriculum. Juan Ramón, however, charts this process of self-definition and growth much more thoroughly. He centers it on dynamic, heightened contemplative participation in the fullness of a vision. Through the efforts of participation in this vision, the poet *realizes* the intricacies of his elemental make up as energized, articulated, ordered, and saved by poetry. The poetic exercise simultaneously externalizes the secrets found in internal searches, achieves that destiny manifested through purposeful acts, and opens up eternity by perpetuating the intensity of the moment. Even if Florit's quest for harmony or serenity leads him to plateaux of spiritual achievement in which his own success inhibits further ascents, the pursuit of «su verdad», and the intent to live by it, amount to a solid endorsement of Juan Ramón's more comprehensive formulation of the way to «gracia» and «gloria».

IV

COLLOQUY WITH JOSE LEZAMA LIMA

During the second half of 1937 José Lezama Lima participated in the publication of *Verbum,* the «Organo Oficial de la Asociación Nacional de Estudiantes de Derecho», and turned it into the first in a fruitful series of short-lived literary magazines, which finally led to the sustained and influential publication of *Orígenes* (1944-1956). The three issues of *Verbum* serve as good indicators of the rate at which Juan Ramón's contributions were being made public in La Habana, and of his close liaison with Lezama. Among the four articles and two notes of the first issue (June 1937), we can find, under the title of «Brazo Español», four of Juan Ramón's lyrical portraits of Spanish painters which later appeared in *Españoles de tres mundos,* and also Lezama's first essay of literary criticism, entitled «El secreto de Garcilaso», with a dedication to Juan Ramón Jiménez; among the notes there is one by Lezama on the «Fundación de un estudio libre de pintura y escultura». In the second issue (August 1937), together with two articles, two notes, and a selection of poetry by eight Cuban poets, we can find Juan Ramón's *apuntes* on «Límite del progreso», the last one of which carries a dedication to Lezama; this issue also contains poetry by Lezama and Florit. Finally, among the five articles and six notes of the third and last issue (November 1937), we find a review of Lezama's «Muerte de Narciso» by Angel Gaztelu, and under the title of «Gracia eficaz de Juan Ramón y su visita a nuestra poesía», Lezama's appraisal of *Verso y prosa para niños* and *La poesía cubana en 1936.*[1]

«El secreto de Garcilaso» (A Juan Ramón Jiménez), «Gracia eficaz de Juan Ramón y su visita a nuestra poesía», and, finally, the *tour de*

[1] Other Cuban literary magazines and reviews of general interest also disseminated numerous contributions by Juan Ramón. That very same year of 1937 *Revista Cubana* published three contributions; *Ultra,* four; *Universidad de la Habana,* one. They included two instalments of fragments «De mi 'Diario poético'», three lectures, the prologue of Florit's *Doble acento* under the title of «El único estilo de Eugenio Florit», a transcription of the introductory statement and the poetry read during the radio broadcast of «Ciego ante ciegos», and the text of his opening speech for the inauguration of the «Festival de la poesía cubana».

force of «Coloquio con Juan Ramón Jiménez» (first published in the
January 1938 issue of *Revista cubana,* but dated as finished in June 1937),
constitute the most visible part of Lezama's prose output before 1940,
placing the beginning of Lezama's career as critic, essayist, and poetic
theorist in close relationship with his exposure to the visiting Spanish
master.

«El secreto de Garcilaso» amounts to Lezama's contribution to the
debates that classify poets and poetry by their affinity either to the
accessible work of Lope, or to the elitist and hermetic work of Góngora.
To this polarization, discussed and revisited by many since Dámaso
Alonso and Vossler, Lezama adds a reappraisal of the position of Garcilaso as the poet who had manifested in the sixteenth century a synthesis
of both seventeenth-century extremes.

The discussion covers many angles and issues in which Lezama's
complex poetics start to take shape in directions that are not strictly
related to Juan Ramón's way of thinking. But insofar as Lezama uses the
polarization as a point of departure, one is struck by the similarity
with Juan Ramón's use of such polarity in his already mentioned appraisal
of Florit's *Doble acento,* and in his subsequent discussion (1948) of «Lo
'fable' y lo 'inefable'», and «Dos líneas permanentes de la poesía española», two sections of his series of lectures entitled «Poesía abierta y
poesía cerrada».[2] In these critical pieces, Juan Ramón uses the polar
classification first to frame his positive evaluation of the contrapuntal
voices in Florit's poetry. Later, he uses it more polemically to separate
what he regarded as the best (poesía abierta, romance español, el primer
romancero, Gil Vicente, Juan de la Cruz, el Lope más lírico, Bécquer, lo
inefable, lo esencial) from what he regarded as not so good (poesía
cerrada, préstamos afrancesados o italianizantes, los *Cancioneros* de cor-
te, Garcilaso, Fray Luis, Góngora, Calderón, Gracián, los neoclásicos
del XVIII, los académicos del XIX, lo fable, lo sustancial).[3] This polemic
sifting contains a good dose of valid critical insight with respect to the
championed side of the lists —«poesía abierta», Bécquer, etc.—; the
aciertos, however, are sadly overshadowed by the weight of Juan Ramón's
subtextual but unsubtle abuse directed against so many living poets he
would decidedly line up with the not-so-good, in order to include them
in the target of his dismissal. His repeated disclaimer to this effect actually
functions like a sardonic reminder that he is talking about the unmen-
tioned poets: «Cito sólo poetas muertos», «De los vivos tampoco hablo».[4]

---

[2] According to the chronology included in *Juan Ramón Jiménez: El escritor
y la crítica,* Aurora de Albornoz, ed. (Madrid, 1980), pp. 343-49, «Poesía abierta
y poesía cerrada» was first delivered in Montevideo during Jiménez's highly
successful visit of 1948.

[3] «Poesía abierta y poesía cerrada» [1948], *El trabajo gustoso (Conferencias)*
(México, 1961), pp. 83-115.

[4] *El trabajo gustoso,* p. 101.

Lezama's use of the polarization as a point of departure is more engaging, as his choice of foci, Garcilaso *vis à vis* Góngora, introduces and documents one of Lezama's major distinctions. Under the subtitle of «Orbe poético de Góngora y penetración ambiental en Garcilaso» he writes:

> Debemos distinguir orbe poético de aire pleno, de ambiente poético. El primero comporta una señal de mando por la que todas las cosas al sumergirse en él son obligadas a obediencia ciega, aquietadas por un nuevo sentido regidor. Orbe poético —ya en el caso de Góngora, ya en el de la mística del siglo XVI, que se va apoderando de las cosas, de las palabras, quedando detenidos por la sorpresa de esa aprehensión repentina que las va a destruir eléctricamente, para sumergirlas en un amanecer en el que ellas mismas no se reconozcan. Animales, ángeles y vegetales, fines en su impenetrabilidad, en su sueño desesperante, son dentro de la red de un orbe poético, medios ciegos por la impetuosidad de la nueva unidad que los encierra. (...) Formado por el poeta el orbe poético es arrastrado por él; en ocasiones (...) creerá romperlo, dominarlo, detenerlo cuando quiera. La obligación para con él es dura, el trabajo desesperado, la obediencia ciega.[5]

The making of an *orbe poético,* in this case associated with Góngora's way of writing poetry, involves the same all-inclusive motions Juan Ramón delineated as essential in the making of his *Obra.* My previous discussion of «Intelijencia, dame» and «Cielo» could be recast to document the ways in which the *orbe poético* «repossesses things and words leaving them suspended by the surprise of that sudden apprehension that destroys them electrically to submerge them in a dawn in which the very words and things will not recognize themselves».[6] For Juan Ramón the surprise lies in the perfect match between word and thing after the recovery of their forgotten relationship; for Lezama, the surprise opens the way to such a new appreciation of the words, the things and the names, that their new significance obliterates the relative meaninglessness of the old. This process of revitalization at the level of the basic components of poetic expression —metaphor, image, word— helpfully dissects and analyses the internal motions necessary for the building of a poetic system. Through the revitalization of these building-blocks, Juan Ramón, and many other poets, construct or order what Cole defines as the «magnificent edifice of ideas» that makes the world «fit for a God to inhabit». Lezama's poetry, insofar as it can be caricatured as even more hermetic and baroque than Góngora's, has next to nothing to do with Juan Ramón's, and yet Lezama's focus on the concept of *orbe poético* clearly points to interests shared in their ways of thinking about poetry.

The title of Lezama's review of the then recently released *Verso y*

---

[5] «El secreto de Garcilaso», *Obras completas,* II, pp. 16-17.
[6] My translation of Lezama as quoted above.

prosa para niños and *La poesía cubana en 1936,* already includes the full thrust of the tribute which the article as a whole represents. «Gracia eficaz de Juan Ramón y su visita a nuestra poesía» fully denotes the impact of the Spanish master on the Cuban poets that came to him. «Efficacious grace» has a specific Roman Catholic meaning which must not be overlooked if we are to understand the weight of the compliment. This kind of grace is inevitably followed by the effect for which it is intended; it is a passing or temporary help given to perform some particular act; its short duration makes it distinct from the permanent «sanctifying or habitual grace», just as the inevitability of its effect makes it distinct from «sufficient grace» which, being enough to occasion the act in question, still might be rendered inefficacious as a result of the resistance of the recipient.[7] With the choice of that theological technicality, easily camouflaged as a mere resonant combination of adjective and noun, Lezama acknowledges that Juan Ramón irresistibly caused the poetic ferment around him.

The article calls attention to the opportunities offered by reading the works of Juan Ramón as specifically useful in clarifying many of the issues and difficulties faced by those involved in poetic exploration:

> Hoy que podemos recoger la regalía de que uno de los grandes líricos contemporáneos, insertado en uno de los momentos más eficaces y universales de la poesía española, toque esenciales problemas de la sensibilidad cubana, meditemos en el secreto y claridad de su palabra (...)[8]

Continuing to use a collective first person which, rather than being a rhetorical device, is intended to include all the Cuban poets that shared the quickening induced by Juan Ramón's visit, Lezama portrays the irruption of the master on the Cuban scene as something akin to the coming of a saviour:

> Contemplábamos fríamente cómo hoy la poesía recorre las más opuestas etapas, de la tragedia del lenguaje a la expresión de la angustia, rabiosamente temporal, fuera del toque de la gracia. (...)
>
> Habíamos huido de las seguridades elementales y necesarias de los ojos, nos fijábamos en el acto naciente y en la redención por la gracia, porque quizá la tragedia del lenguaje y la angustia de la culpa fuesen formas del conocer con los ojos. Y aquí podemos encajar la claridad y dulce luz y la gracia en vagos ángeles, esperada claridad hasta el sueño y la luz, leve humedad de ámbito refractado, de Juan Ramón Jiménez (...)[9]

Lezama's own meditation on the value of having such an auspicious presence available takes the issue of «grace» and elaborates it, interpret-

[7] For a brief discussion of these theological distinctions see under «grace» in Van A. Harvey's *A Handbook of Theological Terms* (New York, 1964).
[8] «Gracia eficaz (...)», *Verbum,* 1, no. 3 (November 1937), p. 62.
[9] «Gracia eficaz (...)», p. 58.

ing Juan Ramón's contribution in terms of how his poetry makes this grace available:

> Porque esta poesía que cuenta entre lo suyo una invocación al mar del sur en abril, cierra su círculo órfico pidiéndole a la inteligencia el nombre exacto de las cosas. Colocada frente a la más decisiva prueba marina y a la dominadora presencia de los nombres, la gracia podía fluir sus compases, mecedora de su seguro ámbito, mover diestramente sus hojas. La gracia se hacía eficaz y palpable en las puntualidades del encuentro, burlando la zancadilla de Satán; pues ésta, la gracia, permite al éxtasis de adelantarse al encuentro, recibir un agrado producto de los dictados del reverso, del misterioso detrás de las palabras escogidas. La finalidad de las pesquisas de esta gracia consistía en habitar el momento aún firmemente existente en que no se podían definir las enemistades, en que la resolución lineal y unida de la poesía rehusaba los soportes del aislamiento o el nutrimiento falso del distinguir o excluir, aprovechaba tan sólo el fulgor momentáneo de ese centro medusario que sumerge a las palabras en una nueva experiencia nocturna. La contemplación de esa gracia producía la plástica interna del poema, y su secreto asegurado parecía mantenernos en el aprovechamiento irremplazable de su inicial.[10]

In Lezama's formulation —canonically in tune with Catholic orthodoxy— only grace allows the poet, and by extension the reader of poetry, to inhabit that moment of intensity in which the unitive resolution granted by the clear vision keeps all threatening and alienating animosities at bay. The use of the term «grace» remains richly ambiguous throughout, in ways also consonant with traditional doctrinal ambiguity: «grace» may be related to an influence —seminal? baptismal? pentecostal?— that issues from Juan Ramón, just as it may be a benefit earned by his poetic endeavours. Whether gratuitous gift or merited benefit, this grace may also be the in-fluence, or benefit shared by those who come into contact either with Juan Ramón's grace-inducing poetry, or with his efficacious way of prodding incipient poets to participate in any of those poetically habitual or sanctifying practices that maximize the benefits or gifts.

The terms «encuentros» and «pesquisas» stand as very clear correlatives of terms already used with reference to Juan Ramón: the effort exerted in bringing oneself to attention, in searching for the concordance of thing, word, name and meaning, in surrendering to the luminosity of the vision, constitute a «pesquisa», and the re-suscitation arrived at, whether yielded or gained, constitutes an «encuentro».[11]

Futhermore, with his reference to the «puntualidades del encuentro», Lezama speaks of the way in which Juan Ramón's poetry captures, preserves, and keeps available the essences extracted from the circumstan-

---

[10] «Gracia eficaz (...)», pp. 58-59.
[11] Cf.: Cortázar's elaborate and sustained use of the terms «búsqueda» and «encuentro», which might not be altogether unrelated to Lezama's no less involved exploration of parallel issues.

tiality of time's flux. The grace in question acquires its efficacy and palpability mostly because of its reliable punctuality in yielding what comes to be regarded as a «secreto asegurado». The secret remains hidden, but its presence is felt dependably there by virtue of the poet's capacity to voice its address: the coordinates that tell us where it lives, and make evident how it speaks to us.

Resuscitations, epiphanies, *encuentros,* are all made available by Juan Ramón in ways that fully satisfy Lezama's most rigorous requisites for poetry, most clearly expressed in his «Exámenes» of 1950:

> Un sistema poético del mundo puede reemplazar a la religión, se constituye en religión. Ese fue el esplendor de aquel *quia absurdum,* porque es absurdo, del catolicismo de los primeros siglos. Si la metáfora como fragmento y la imagen como incesante evaporación, logran establecer las coordenadas entre su absurdo y su gravitación, tendríamos el nuevo sistema poético, es decir, la más segura marcha hacia la religiosidad de un cuerpo que se restituye y se abandona a su misterio. El que logre disolver, decía un experimentalista como el canciller Bacon, que no podía olvidar la alquimia, la mirra en la sangre, vencerá el tiempo. Si la poesía logra disolver la mirra en la sangre, es decir, la alabanza, en la circunstancialidad de la sangre, el espíritu renacerá de nuevo en la alegría creada.[12]

The basic constituents of poetry, image and metaphor, Lezama claims, rearrange words in new contexts that appear absurd as the incongruity of their new juxtaposition challenges old expectations conventionally stimulated by their common associations. This absurdity, this apparent disconnectedness is equivalent to the new nocturnal experience in which words are submerged,[13] and to the electrically destructive immersion of words and things in a dawn in which they do not recognize themselves.[14] If the absurdity provided by the apparently incongruous juxtaposition serves as the cleansing darkness or fluid («noche oscura», destructive electricity, engulfing waters) that rids the words of their detritus, their re-emergence beyond absurdity makes evident a meaning or a vision hitherto inaccesible, «producto de los dictados del reverso, del misterioso detrás de las palabras escogidas».[15]

Lezama sees the poet involved in a constant «pesquisa» for those new arrangements which are neither haphazard nor accidental, but which depend on the «gravitation» that cleansed words exert over one another for the sake of that new birth of meaning. The extent and rigour of these «pesquisas» reveal their full complexity with the realization that the crafting and controlling of these cleansing and revelatory images and

---

[12] *Obras completas,* II, p. 227.
[13] «Gracia eficaz (...)», p. 59; quoted above.
[14] *Obras completas,* II, p. 16; quoted above.
[15] «Gracia eficaz (...)», p. 58; quoted above.

metaphors has to be expanded and contained within the all-inclusive margins of an *orbe poético.*

In Juan Ramón's «Cielo», for instance, the initial forgetfulness of the speaker jars against the common-sensical conception that it is impossible to forget the «cielo». The absurdity of juxtaposing the ever present «cielo» with the forgetfulness of it, challenges conventional associations, and opens the way for a more attentive encounter with the meanings at the core of the word. Only this core, then, exerts its proper gravitational pull towards the new vision. The poem repeatedly acts like a formula for finding the fullness of the vision, like an address for locating and inhabiting the richness of the moment. The ecstatic exclamation at the end —«y te has ido elevando hasta tu nombre!»— repeatedly functions like a psalm of praise and thanksgiving, through which the threats of time have been overcome by dissolving myrrh in the blood, *alabanzas* in circumstantiality; through the new suscitation of the forgotten «cielo», the created joy rekindles the spirit.[16]

«Coloquio con Juan Ramón Jiménez» has always been regarded as the most significant point of contact between Lezama and Juan Ramón. Some thirty years after the fact Lezama explains how one of the meetings that led to the publication of *La poesía cubana en 1936* actually triggered his desire to write the fictional interview with Juan Ramón:

> Convocó por los periódicos a una reunión en el Lyceum y esa reunión fue sin duda la gloria de su visita. De ahí salió mi «Coloquio con Juan Ramón Jiménez», y mi afán de mostrar el mundo hipertélico de la poesía, como la poesía es un en sí que al mismo tiempo va mucho más allá de su finalidad. Era ejemplar ver como aquel hombre se acercaba a la poesía de los demás fueran principiantes, desconocidos o simples seres errantes con un destino subdividido. Esperaba siempre como una gran sorpresa, mi frase para definirlo o encontrarlo sería *asombro sosegado en écstasis,* la infinitud de un gozo en el encuentro con el niño de la poesía.[17]

In the fictional dialogue Lezama honours and engages the older poet, casting him in the role of Socratic teacher. In doing so, Lezama also creates and adopts the role of the disciple who fulfils the ultimately more active function of Platonic interlocutor and transcriber of the exchange. Juan Ramón never received such a comprehensive tribute from his Spanish disciples; nor did he ever feel compelled to voice his acceptance of such a tribute in more positive terms than those of his already quoted endorsement.[18]

In the introduction to the dialogue, Lezama concentrates on a eulogiz-

---

[16] *Obras completas,* II, p. 227; quoted above.
[17] «El momento cubano de Juan Ramón Jiménez», p. 10, col. 3.
[18] «Nota» by Juan Ramón Jiménez to preface Lezama's «Coloquio con Juan Ramón Jiménez», *Obras completas,* II, p. 44; quoted above in pp. 16-17. See also *Juan Ramón Jiménez en Cuba,* p. 155.

ing comparison of the innovativeness of Juan Ramón's and Picasso's habits of growing within their respective artistic practices.

> Picasso dice: «No busco, encuentro.» Juan Ramón dice: «No estudio, aprendo.» Aprendieron encontrando, modo también de la serpiente de cristal, saliendo siempre de su piel, sus últimas adquisiciones. Por eso, si buscamos en ellos las distintas maneras que han atravesado, nos perdemos; sorprendemos sólo una experiencia sensible aislada. Su legitimidad nos obliga a descubrir en ellos lo más valioso, lo que es en sí curiosa obra de arte, fuerza creacional, riqueza infantil de creación. Para ellos, la manera, el estilo han sido últimas etapas de largas corrientes producidas por organismos vivientes de expresión. Mientras que los más (temed al hombre de una sola experiencia sensible victoriosa) alcanzaron una manera y la degeneraron en manía; una tradición fraccionada, y se apresuraron a convertirla en ley.
>
> Juan Ramón, Picasso. Su fidelidad radica sólo en el acoplamiento de la virtud aprehensiva volcada sobre el objeto provocador en el momento en que éste ofrecía el mejor de sus cuerpos, como en la cita final. Su secreto, su primer acercamiento a las claves y a lo eterno, permanecen intactos.[19]

This comparison of the two masters leads to a crucial qualification of Lezama's claim about the reliability of poetry —and art— as grace-inducing practices. When Lezama talks about establishing coordinates between the absurdity and the gravitation of metaphor and image («Exámenes»), or when he refers to the punctual accessibility of grace («Gracia eficaz...»), he seems to be assigning to poetry a quasi-mathematically charted reliability, of the kind most often reserved for the sciences, or the most consistent philosophical syntheses. In «Coloquio...», however, Lezama ascribes the successive, repeated and reliable newness of each achievement of Picasso and Juan Ramón to the masters' capacity to confront each new inciting experience, with an artistic consciousness completely denuded of accumulated artifice. If the poetry of Juan Ramón provides access and impetus for his own and our own revitalizing experiences, with a degree of reliability that can been regarded as quasi-mathematically charted, the motions remain refreshing and compelling by a successiveness and a reliability that is not merely formulaic, or rigidly catechistic. Those repeated approaches to the available resuscitation, and the assurance that they remain accessible, must never sink into the overconfident expectation of a predictable laboratory result, nor into the ritual complacency of devotional religiosity. To respond adequately to the obligation of discovering in this kind of poetry that which is most worthwhile —what Lezama suggests and what Juan Ramón would endorse— the reader has to surrender repeatedly to the fresh emulation of the original encounter and the original surprise. Emulating the mastery of this habit of innocence —«la infinitud de su gozo en el encuentro con el niño de la poesía»— the reader also acquires that cutaneous nimbleness of the per-

---

[19] *Obras completas*, II, p. 45.

petually skin-sloughing crystal serpent ascribed to Juan Ramón and Picasso.

The skin-shedding metaphor for growing, both artistically and spiritually, can be seen as related to Juan Ramón's advice regarding the necessary direction of self-awareness and growth. With reference to the central issue of the *coloquio,* «la insularidad», Lezama and his fictional Juan Ramón soon arrive at the importance of searching within oneself, and within the heart of one's cultural or national origins:

> Yo: (...) La resaca no es otra cosa que el aporte que las islas pueden dar a las corrientes marinas, mientras que los trabajos de incorporación se lastran en un bizantinismo cuyo límite está en producir en el litoral un falso espejismo de escamas podridas, en crucigramas viciosos.
>
> J.R.J.: Cuestión de ondas. Por eso insisto e insistiré siempre en la internación, la vida hacia el centro, única manera de legitimarse. Ustedes han estado más atentos a los barcos que les llegaban que al trabajo de su resaca.[20]

In this exchange, Juan Ramón concurs with Lezama's call for yet another act of cleansing, in this case a coastal scouring. Emphasizing the importance of the purging undertow, and calling it the contribution islands can really offer to the surrounding currents and open seas, both poets agree that the island, the isolated creative sensibility, must not be defined by what surrounds it, nor by the adherences brought by those surroundings, but rather by the way the island stands against engulfment. Juan Ramón uses this observation to expand on the need for this isolated creative sensibility, be it national or individual, to define itself merely in terms of what it possesses within. This call for internalization which Lezama makes Juan Ramón utter is yet another admission that the principal object of knowledge lies, for the individual, within the space delimited or appropriated by the expanding self, and for the national or cultural entity, within the headwaters of its origins and the margins of its historical development. This could very well serve as a point of departure for an argument that one of the central concerns of the group of Cuban poets gathered around Lezama, the search for *orígenes,* received significant encouragement from Juan Ramón's insistence on seeking for roots and bone marrow.

Much of the forcefulness of the «Coloquio...» depends precisely on Lezama's creation of a socratic Juan Ramón who advises on the importance of looking at one's own origins, even as he represents the most formidable of external influences. The disciple masterfully elaborates the irony of forcing the teacher to deliver the most sought-after lesson on independence, without distorting it beyond what even Juan Ramón would recognize as his.

[20] *Obras completas,* II, p. 50.

The dialogue becomes more explicit as the participants assess some of the implications of writing as a Cuban or as a Spaniard.

> Yo: (...) Nosotros, insulares, hemos vivido sin religiosidad, bajo especie de pasajeros accidentes, y no es nuestra arrogancia lo que menos nos puede conducir al ridículo. Hemos carecido de orgullo de expresión, nos hemos recurvado al vicio, que es elegancia en la geometría desligada de la flor, y la obra de arte no se da entre nosotros como una exigencia subterrígena, sino como una frustración de la vitalidad.
>
> J.R.J. Tal vez puedan ustedes alcanzar así una alegría que no les adormezca la inquietud, y una elegancia, como usted dice, que no sea el refugio rencoroso de lo que no se ha tocado o despertado.[21]

That «frustration of vitality», which Lezama regards as the source or impetus of Cuban writing at that point, is another label for what he identified in «Gracia eficaz de Juan Ramón (...)» as a poetry «fuera del toque de gracia». Nevertheless, immediately after this negative dictum, Lezama makes Juan Ramón hope that Cuba as a whole, and its creators in particular, might be able to achieve a dynamically balanced state of grace which would yield what Lezama calls in another previously quoted context «a rebirth into created joy», while at the same time avoiding a fall into lethargic complacent contentment. The hope also demands that expression should develop towards a noble elegance, completely unrelated to the reactive stance of those who oppose to their sense of lack and incapacity, a desensitizing arrogant grudge.

The dialogue ends with Juan Ramón's advice, specifically targeted for attentive apprentices:

> En sus años jóvenes, el poeta puede y debe aprender en todos los países y más en los que en el momento de su despertar viven en la plenitud de la expresión poética. (...) Pero una vez orientado en su camino ideal, el poeta consciente vuelve en espíritu y forma a su patria. Si yo he usado tanto el romance, la canción y el verso desnudo, no ha sido por una sugestión técnica. La poesía española sigue desarrollándose, es claro, en sustancia, como ninguna otra que yo conozca, y su forma no es nunca arquitectura externa ni juego ingenioso, aunque también haya de esto en lo popular español, sino gracia sucesiva, en todos los sentidos de la gracia, y la gracia poética mayor del mundo. Y esa forma poética que yo amo tanto, por española y por graciosa, es, a mi juicio, la forma de la verdadera aristocracia humana española, tipo acabado de lo natural y lo reflexivo, que tanto se encuentra en el pueblo español.[22]

Lezama chooses to close the exchange bringing to mind Juan Ramón's ideal of an aristocracy based on its naturalness and its capacity for reflexion; as the Juan Ramón created by Lezama is allowed to cast this ideal in its real or imagined Spanish manifestation, we realize that this

---

[21] *Obras completas,* II, p. 61.
[22] *Obras completas,* II, p. 64.

model is precisely what they both hope the Cubans, or anybody else, will emulate in their own way, as they grow towards their own created joy, and their own noble elegance of sui-generis expression —their own way of swelling their own «inmensa minoría». Florit's overexposure to Juan Ramón's magnetism, for instance, yielded a derivative poetry that inhibited whichever pursuits he might have followed more in tune with specifically Cuban or individual directions. Lezama, on the other hand, developing his utterly unjuanramonian and idiosyncratic poetry, actually remained closer to the spirit of the master's demands for one's own forays into one's own *orígenes.*

THE EXAMINATION OF CINTIO VITIER

So far I have reviewed the contacts and confluences of Juan Ramón with Florit and Lezama, more or less up to the point of the master's departure for the United States in 1939, after spending two years in La Habana. Vitier's contacts with Juan Ramón until then were also important, as they reveal much about Juan Ramón's practice of his mastership. But in terms of what traces one poet might have left in the other, the significance of their *confluencia* during the two-year visit is much more limited than in the case of Florit and Lezama. Nevertheless, the case of Vitier's relationship with Jiménez and his poetry acquires renewed interest after Vitier's exposure to Juan Ramón's American poetry, particularly «Espacio» and «Animal de fondo». Since my coverage of this belated but significant area of confluence will be included in my discussion of the poetry of the late 1940s and the 1950s, the following section on Vitier up to 1939 will of necessity be brief.

We have to rely on Vitier's own account of his meeting with Juan Ramón Jiménez. The lyrical texture of the memoir stands as a good indicator of the adolescent's excitement and the master's didactic demeanor; all tenderly remembered. Once more the visiting model poet reads, decides what is good-better-and-best, suggests a title, and consents to the continuation of yet another poetic vocation.

«El examen»

Había mandado él a cortar mis papeles de un tamaño que a mí me pareció, no sé por qué, precioso e importante. Algo dijo de su gusto por el orden, y en su modo de decirlo yo sentía la lección de pureza, de distinción, de apartamiento: una galería de estancias ordenadas por la poesía...

(¡Qué quietas están las cosas
y qué bien se está con ellas!...)

Solos en el comedor vacío del Hotel Vedado (la luz, el mar, los pinos vibrando afuera), su naranjada evocaba para sí, no sé por qué, todo lo que él había puesto en la palabra *sur*. Disponía las páginas cuidadosamente. Por fin sacó, igual que una joya cuya aparente insignificancia no lograba ocultar

51

la materia escogida de que realmente estaba hecha, su lápiz amarillo, único, exacto.

> (Todo dispuesto ya, en su punto
> para la eternidad.
> —¡Qué bien! ¡Cuán bello!
> Guirnalda cotidiana de mi vida...)

Con el lápiz a mano leía en voz intensa, profunda y transparente, mis pobres versos que salían, tropezando como niños mendigos disfrazados de príncipes, a deshacerse en el rayo blanco de la belleza. Con un *1* hermosamente deformado, como la torre o la palmera en el temblor del agua, me calificaba los poemas mejores; con un *2* que era el cisne salvado de los lagos de Darío, me premiaba los poemas peores. Yo iba pasando mi examen como una fiebre atroz, larguísima, dichosa.

Qué tardes infinitas estuvimos allí, seguimos estando allí, sobre la ausente ciudad agradecida, él con el lápiz terrible, divino, yo con mi sangre golpeándome el pecho y las sienes, oscuro, enloquecido de esperanza.

De pronto se levantó, imponente y bondadoso. En un papel insigne había escrito, enlazando las palabras como un enredo de luces y de sueños, el título que le daba a mis nadas primerizas. Y tendiéndome la mano, sin testigos, con la majestad llana de su único tribunal insuperable, me dijo: *sí*.[1]

But, despite the exuberant rememberance of «El examen», Vitier's own regard for the poetry composed under Juan Ramón's supervision soon proved to be insufficient:

Pronto empecé a sentirme insatisfecho de aquel libro [*Poemas* (1938)] y a intentar otras formas de expresión más penetradas de mis intuiciones y esperanzas, lo que me fue posible, después de varios años de oscuro desconcierto, a través de la experiencia de esa misma oscuridad y de la lectura de dos poetas objetivamente irreconciliables: José Lezama Lima y César Vallejo.[2]

At this juncture, Vitier chooses to explore his own hopes and intuitions, and to express them in a voice more in tune with the achievements of an older Cuban poet, and an established American master. His decision to resist the magnetism of Juan Ramón's way of making poetry, like Lezama's choice and unlike Florit's, could be regarded as Vitier's way of following Juan Ramón's imperative of looking towards the center. It would be interesting to analyze this unavailable and disowned juvenilia —which Vitier saw fit to exclude from his first retrospective compilation of 1953—, if not for its intrinsic value, at least to document the level of derivativeness evident in those novice texts written under-the-influence

---

[1] «Homenaje a Juan Ramón Jiménez», *Juan Ramón Jiménez: El escritor y la crítica*, pp. 56-57. This «Homenaje» was first read in the Lyceum de la Habana in January of 1957, and first published in *Asomante*, 13, no. 2 (April-June 1957), pp. 31-53.

[2] *Diez poetas cubanos: 1937-1957*, Cintio Vitier, ed. and co-author (La Habana, 1948), p. 167.

at the outset of his poetic practice. Despite the acknowledged resistance to the over-bearing influence of the Spanish master —which is not to say that he remained untouched by the efficacious grace—, the earliest of Vitier's poetry generally available in *Vísperas* (1938-1953) opens with a section under the salvaged title Juan Ramón had given Vitier for his earliest and now disowned efforts: «Luz ya sueño».[3]

In this section, dated between 1938 and 1942, despite so much that already manifests seriously engaged readings of Vallejo and Lezama, there is still much that remains infused with a good number of the concerns also evident in Juan Ramón's work. «Humo» is the very first poem of *Vísperas*:

Mi deseo se vuelve
un delicado bosque,
un enigma de nubes.
Ahora no quiero nada
sino mirar, beber
el oro de las hojas
nevadas de tristeza.
¿Qué es el mundo? La vida
rumorosa me ciega.
¿Quién acaba de huir
de tu mirada trémula?
¿Qué dios o qué recuerdo?
¿Qué pájaro? Mi oído
tañe su oscura forma:
verdes árboles, rayos
de callada dulzura
suenan... ¡Cuándo sabremos
el himno de aquel humo
silencioso que huye!

(*Vísperas*, p. 11)

The questioning already betrays the habits of a seeker, and the rest of the poem declares that the search is to be directed towards «my desire», that internal, elusive, risk-ridden part of the self portrayed as smoke, as a dissipating enigma. Reconcentrating that sense of dissipation, focussing on the flight of the blinding smoke, perhaps by looking to the fire and the fuel that produce it, could very well turn out to be the clarifying defogging experience of self-knowledge. The final exclamation of the poem thrives on the urgency of the lack of knowledge, but as it names precisely what is not yet known, the naming becomes a pointer towards the requisite end, and the requisite hymn is already halfway sung as the voice chokes in the confession of its need to sing it.

The hymn that needs to be sung would sound much like what Leza-

---

[3] «El examen» above, and «El momento cubano de Juan Ramón Jiménez», p. 9, col. 2.

ma calls an «alabanza» dissolved in «la circunstancialidad de la sangre».[4] Thus we see Vitier, from the very first piece of his first comprehensive collection, already interested in processes of regeneration beyond present states of disintegration and loss. His way up involves the singing of a hymn, and with this, he places poetry —like Lezama, and Juan Ramón— at the center of those processes of regeneration.

The poem «Otoño», from the same initial section, could be regarded as one of those regenerating hymns about regeneration —this one to be sung at matins:

> Respiro. La verdad
> de la vida me baña de silencio.
> Se filtra el sol por las persianas
> y recuerdo la luz, como otra vida
> que sólo he vislumbrado.
> Quizá este minuto lo recuerde
> también en la callada lejanía
> en que tiempo y espacio se confunden,
> como el sonido y la ilusión
> en la palabra. ¿Qué silencio,
> qué palabra, qué luz nunca gozada
> resplandece en el lecho de este río
> de mi vida, más dulce que el otoño
> dorando en la penumbra la memoria?
> ¡Oh tesoro de paz, vida divina,
> transparencia de amor, en que perduro!
>
> (*Vísperas*, p. 19)

If Vitier's poem resembles any other poem in theme and vocabulary, it is Jorge Guillén's «Mientras el aire es nuestro»:

> Respiro,
> Y el aire en mis pulmones
> Ya es saber, ya es amor, ya es alegría.
> (...)

Both poets focus on two of the most often repeated, and most often ignored fundamental motions, breathing and waking, and lift them to the status of miracles that suscitate a fully comprehensive revelation. That revelation energizes the being attentive to the miraculous implication of the normal, well beyond the level usually reached by the natural efficacy of breathing and awakening.

So many other poets have written comparable statements about the effects of the observance of miraculous normality, epiphanies, and regeneration, and most of them intend to instill in the reader a comparable disposition to attentiveness, revelation, and renewal. Even if Jorge Gui-

---

[4] LEZAMA, *Obras completas*, II, p. 227; quoted above.

llén belongs to the Juanramonian lineage, it would be unjustified to suggest that Juan Ramón is principally or solely responsible for the pursuit of this line of reflection in any of his disciples. Nevertheless, that Vitier's earliest poetry evidences these kinds of issues does demonstrate that the master and one of the youngest of his Cuban novices shared concerns that must have nurtured their contacts.

VI

JUAN RAMON AFTER 1936: «CAMINO MUNDO ARRIBA»

Before 1936 Juan Ramón's ideas about successive spiritual growth had been based on an ever-increasing incorporation of beauty within the vital space of the poet, and on an ever-increasing capacity to salvage the intensity of the moment through his poetry. These aesthetic approaches to the metaphysical issues raised by his immersion in the realm of nature, excluded or at least did not evidently express, much of what others like Unamuno, Ortega, and the younger poets of the Generation of 27 were expressing in explicitly religious, social, ethical and political terms. During his Caribbean sojourn, however, Juan Ramón started to voice his opinions about literary, political, social, and ethical issues in ways that represent a break with his previously held reluctance to be engaged in extra-poetic matters. The events of the Civil War, for instance, became topics of constant concern during his years in Puerto Rico and Cuba, and his public statements at that juncture proved him a much more avowed Republican than had been expected given his lack of political involvement in Spain before 1936. Some of the other issues that started to attract his attention also evidence the nature of his new directions; among these we can list his positive attitude to manual and intellectual work,[1] his statements about the need to develop an aristocracy of «sencillos seres de profundo cultivo interior» engaged in what he called «comunismo idealista, lírico subjetivo»,[2] and his denunciation of an unnecessarily gadget-cluttered society.[3]

Juan Ramón's first contribution to what later became the body of his specifically ethical teachings dates from June of 1936, and was prepared for a public reading at the Residencia de Estudiantes. The title,

---

[1] Cf.: «El trabajo gustoso» (1936). In conversation with Graciela Palau de Nemes, discussing the range of Jiménez's interest in non-poetical matters, the biographer pointed out that his ethical and political concerns were expressed as early as *Platero y yo*. The point is well taken, even as I insist that the most explicit manifestations of these concerns are to be found in Juan Ramón's work after 1936.

[2] «El hombre inmune» (1937), *La corriente infinita*, p. 277.

[3] «Límite del progreso», *Verbum*, 1, no. 2 (July-August 1937), pp. 3-11.

«Política poética» —later changed to «El trabajo gustoso»—, had promised to reveal a new facet of Jiménez's thought, which would finally clarify his commitment —or lack thereof— with respect to the mounting tensions of the few months before the outbreak of the Civil War.

The lecture was delivered, but not by Juan Ramón.[4] His refusal to appear in public on this occasion could be interpreted as another of his polemical tantrums, or as a genuine product of his long-standing aversion to audiences. In any case, four months later, Juan Ramón Jiménez breaks with his old reluctance to appear in public, and reads «El trabajo gustoso» in Río Piedras, Puerto Rico. Once in Cuba, he read the same lecture again, and soon made himself available to deliver two new pieces. The contents of these lectures, and other statements in which Juan Ramón's new non-aesthetical didacticism comes to the fore will be discussed later, together with Vitier's appraisal of their impact. For now, suffice it to say that Juan Ramón's first lecture shows publicly his interests in issues other than the purest poetry, and that his Puerto Rican debut as a lecturer inaugurates that period of unprecedented public exposure which made him accessible to the young poets who chose to come to him.

The directions of Juan Ramón's works after 1936 could be charted as a basically straightforward progression of his critical prose towards the ethical demands of his *Política poética*,[5] and of his poetry towards the mystical stance of *Animal de fondo* and *Dios deseado y deseante*. The following two excerpts serve as adequate representations of what could be regarded as a manifesto of the late Juan Ramón:

> «Política» entiendo que es administración material, total e ideal. Y a la política se debe ir, por tanto, con vocación auténtica, como a la poesía, admi-

---

[4] While GRACIELA PALAU DE NEMES (1957) points out that «El 8 de octubre de 1936 el poeta leyó, por segunda vez en su vida, una conferencia, la misma que había leído en España antes de su partida» (p. 296). FRANCISCO GARFIAS in his introduction to *El trabajo gustoso*, p. 11, gives more substantial details on this point: «Es el 15 de junio de 1936 cuando por primera vez, a instancias de amigos y admiradores, se decide a leer en la Residencia de Estudiantes, en Madrid, su 'Política poética'. Pero a última hora se arrepiente. Los periódicos, al día siguiente, dirán que el poeta, 'impedido por causas ajenas a su voluntad de presentarse ante el auditorio, había encomendado la lectura de su trabajo a uno de sus discípulos predilectos'.»

[5] The body of Juan Ramón's non-lyrical prose writings started to appear organised in book-length presentations with the posthumous publication of *El trabajo gustoso (Conferencias)* [México], and *La corriente infinita (Crítica y evocación)* [Madrid], both edited and introduced by FRANCISCO GARFIAS, and released by Aguilar simultaneously in 1961. As recently as 1982, GERMÁN BLEIBERG reorganised many of these prose writings into a one-volume edition under the title of *Política poética* —the original title of Jiménez's very first lecture now known as «El trabajo gustoso». The organization of Bleiberg's edition depends on a substantial table of contents in which Juan Ramón himself itemised what he intended to publish under that title as part of his projected rearrangement of *la obra*.

nistración total también y ejemplo de todas las otras actividades morales superiores.

(...) La unión final de todas las grandes obras vocativas, solitarias y gustosas, cumplidas libremente y atadas por el político, es, en suma, la patria cierta.

(...) El poeta y sus equivalentes dan la parte misteriosa que ha de ser lealmente administrada, con el trigo y el pescado, la tela y el papel, el vidrio y la máquina, por el político, eje de todas las elevadas consecuciones benéficas. ¡Y que gran político poético sería el que ascendiera derecho y sin rodeos, en una graduación de esperiencia y conciencia, y rodeado de obras ideales y espirituales, hasta integrarse plenamente con lo material a la mano en su gustosa ilusión![6]

The specifically ethical or political thrust of the previous passage emerges, in the next fragment, in the context of a specifically human quest for divinity.

Mis tres normas vocativas de toda mi vida: la mujer, la obra, la muerte se me resolvieron en conciencia, en compresión del «hasta qué» punto divino podía llegar lo humano de la gracia del hombre; que era lo divino que podía venir por el cultivo; cómo el hombre puede ser hombre último con los dones que hemos supuesto a la divinidad encarnada, es decir, enformada.

Hoy pienso que yo no he trabajado en vano en dios, que he trabajado en dios tanto como he trabajado en poesía.[7]

The common denominators of both passages already establish clear points of contact between the ethical and the mystical directions: if the «político poético» has to ascend his specific secular gradient, the «místico poético» has to climb to his divine point of arrival; if the latter labours to materialise in his flesh the gifts hitherto attributed to the divine, the former has to inform matter in order to achieve the incarnation of his most dear imaginings; both are called to their fullness by their vocation; both improve themselves through the «cultivo», or development, of their «conciencia». The ever-present emphases on the centrality of poetry and beauty now come accompanied by repeated injunctions to work. The task of the seeker becomes much more explicit: seeing, saying and saving have to be supplemented by doing, and while the object of the search is still to achieve successive regenerative discoveries, these are to be arrived at as a response to the vocative specifically addressed to us. In our response to that calling, we realise our fullest measure when we lend our hands to the task of actualising the potentials of whatever part of creation we discover or choose as our sphere of activity.

[6] «Unidad libre», appended as an introduction to «El trabajo gustoso» (1936), *Política poética*, Germán Bleiberg, ed. (Madrid, 1982), pp. 15-16.
[7] Notes to the first edition of *Animal de fondo* (Buenos Aires, 1949), pp. 118-21.

A much-abused modern term could adequately serve to label the full extent of Juan Ramón's demands; he is simply asking for an all-inclusive surrender to the imperatives of consciousness-raising. And if such a term is much over-used and politically vulgarised, the other adequate term that comes to mind turns out to be almost archaic and certainly much too religious: I am referring to the liturgical *sursum corda*. Fortunately, somewhere between the politically over-used raising of consciousness, and the religiously archaic lifting-up of hearts, we can place one of Juan Ramón's images, which incidentally introduces a revealing story of its own:

> Me adorné la ilusión con las liras del sueño y emprendí mi camino mundo arriba.

This is the opening in paragraph form of a poem from «Eternidades» as is appears in *Leyenda* (p. 439).[8] To characterise the full import of Juan Ramón's demands during his latest period by the use of an image from a poem first published in 1918, should seem contradictory in light of the proposition that the ethical and religious terms of the demands were new, and markedly different from his more aesthetic formulations of the second period. Yet, the image «emprendí mi camino mundo arriba» is the product of one of Juan Ramón's most revealing late revisions of his earlier poetry as it shows the extent and nature of his change of emphases. Here is the first stanza of the original poem, as reproduced in *Libros de poesía* (1957):

> Me adorné el corazón
> con las rosas del sueño,
> y emprendí mi camino, azul arriba.
>
> (*LP*, p. 645)

By the time Juan Ramón was working on *Eternidades,* «rosa» and «azul» no longer carried that symbolic specificity so over-worked by the *modernistas.* But even so, this decoration of the heart with the roses of dream or sleep still has echoes of commonplace imagery, and leads to a questionable ascension into the equally commonplace representation of the ideal in the blue of the sky. By contrast, in the *versión revivida,* the juxtaposed terms of «ilusión» and «liras del sueño» introduce a more fruitful consideration of the relationship between the subject's aspirations, and the way in which poetry formulates and qualifies such aspi-

---

[8] *Leyenda,* Antonio Sánchez Romeralo, ed. (Madrid, 1978), is a compendium of Jiménez's poems organised according to a late design for the complete rearrangement of the *obra.* Following Juan Ramón's explicit directions, all the poetry not written in strict or traditional rhymed lines, is printed in paragraph form. This recent compendium represents the best source of «poemas revividos» as well as a new source of «poemas inéditos».

rations. Furthermore, the masterful exchange of «azul arriba» for «mundo arriba» relocates the gradient of transcendence and provides for it a firm foundation, indicating that no matter where ascensions lead, any «camino de perfección» starts on earth.

Both poems —the original as well as its *refundición*— move on to describe the failure of that particular ascent. The first rendition of the failure leads to a farcical expulsion of this new Jacob from the celestial rungs of his ladder, as the stars become leg-swinging vedettes that kick the visionary back to the disordered day of the wakeful:

> Las estrellas estaban
> sentadas todas, niñas desnuditas,
> meciendo sin parar en el azul, las piernas
> en fila, sobre el borde de los cielos.
>
> Llegando yo, me daban, locas
> con los pies en el alma,
> y me echaban, riéndose,
> al día trastornado del despierto.
>
> (*LP,* p. 645)

The description of the failure in the *Leyenda* version still retains much of the original farce; however, the mere deletion of the «niñas desnuditas» already makes the vision much less prurient, while the introduction of the new third stanza, and the alterations to the last one turn the expulsion from the heights into a much more complex statement:

> Y fui encontrándome con las estrellas todas sentadas por las escaleras de lo azul, meciendo sin parar, como ramas, las piernas en el aire del edén.
> Los fondos imprevistos cambiaban, entre ellas, sus luces y sus formas, en una sucesión indefinible, igual que las mareas altas del aguaje, en las siestas eternas de Santiago.
> Llegaba yo, y ellas me daban con los pies en el alma, cayéndose de risa, y me echaban, gritando con loca algarabía de cristales rotos al día trastornado del Moguer no posible del despierto. (*Leyenda,* p. 439)

What the stars inflict on the visionary is not a denial of the validity of his enterprising ascension, but rather a refusal to allow for the complacent enjoyment of his arrival. He is expelled from the inactive state of a pilgrimage concluded in «las siestas de Santiago», and thrown back to the Moguer of his birth, where he must feel compelled to undertake his pilgrimage «mundo arriba» all over again. Relocating himself at his perennial point of departure, ready to start another pilgrimage from the Moguer where all his pilgrimages necessarily start, placing his *campus stellae* before him, provides yet another illuminating context for that repeatedly used motto, Goethe's «Wie das Gestirn, Ohne Hast, Aber ohne Rast».

The specifics of Juan Ramón's trajectory «mundo arriba» have been widely studied by many critics. Most of those studies agree that the mystical formulations of *Dios deseado y deseante* amount to new explorations in heterodox religious terms of concerns for spiritual growth already evident in the works of his second period, from *Diario de un poeta reciéncasado* to *La estación total.* To this we must add that the ethical imperatives presented in his *Política poética,* those demands to participate in «otras actividades morales superiores», have to be regarded as part and parcel of his legacy. Since the scope of this study does not allow for the detailed treatment of Juan Ramón's latest synthesis, I simply recapitulate his most comprehensive lessons by quoting the following categorical statement from the third fragment of «Espacio»:

> Nada es la realidad sin el Destino de una conciencia que la realiza. (*Leyenda,* p. 616)[9]

The aphoristic dictum not only clarifies the relationship between the *conciencia* that has to be developed and the *destino* that has to be fulfilled, but it also offers a possibility to coin yet another name for the project at hand, since «realizar» amounts to «izar lo real».

Before moving on to discuss that part of Lezama's and Vitier's development most clearly related to Juan Ramón's imperatives, this discussion of the master's lesson must close with his own statement:

> I think that this world is our only world, and that in it and with that which is of it, we must acomplish whatever can be accomplished. But why should we not try to make our consciousness contain the infinite universe if it can? The fact that there are poets who have intuitions of infinity is the proof of its existence; and any imagination which is given within man is human. Y am sure that in this world in which we live and die there is an immanent transcendency, and that the poet is the one who can understand, contain, and express that limitless immanence.[10]

---

[9] For an important discussion of Juan Ramón's richly equivocal use of the term «conciencia», specifically in the context of its relationship with the idea of God in *Dios deseado y deseante,* refer to COLE, pp. 82-86. For an equally helpful discussion of Juan Ramón's use of «destino» as «the name of the form of human life», refer to OLSON, p. 170.

[10] Passage translated by OLSON «from a collection of Jiménez's prose writings in the possession of Sr. Don Francisco Hernández-Pinzón Jiménez»; *Circle of Paradox,* p. 194.

VII

FLORIT AFTER 1939: «UN HOMBRE DESVALIDO Y SOLO»

In this attempt to document the different paths pursued by the four authors after Juan Ramón's departure from Cuba, I shall continue with a consideration of Florit's trajectory, regarding it as the most divergently disassociated from what I have presented as confluent in their shared concerns. Through an overview of his poetry written after 1939, I intend to show Florit's adoption of a basically passive stance of resignation, buttressed by a rather conventional static hope in otherworldly redemption. This less-than-positive appraisal of his work and thought should not be regarded as a blanket dismissal of his poetry, but rather as an exploration of his alternative path of development which, in light of the issues at hand, provides a sharp contrast *vis à vis* the more challenging views elaborated by Jiménez, Lezama and Vitier.

José Olivio Jiménez, one of Florit's most enthusiastic critics, asserts the following about his poetry of the Thirties: «Llegamos así al período más intenso y fecundo, el que nos da la imagen más completa, en tanto que artista, de Florit. Son los años de 1930 a 1936».[1] During those years Florit published *Trópico* (1930), and wrote *Doble acento*. Even *Reino* (1938), where the weight of Juan Ramón's influence is most heavily felt, remains outside the boundaries of this optimum period. Since then, Florit had left Cuba for New York, serving as a consular official from 1940 to 1945, and as a professor of Spanish literature at Barnard College after 1945. It can be argued that his departure from Cuba at that juncture is at least partly responsible for his lack of involvement in two very important experiences shared by Lezama and Vitier: first of all, the ferment of the «Grupo de *Orígenes*»,[2] and, subsequently, the social, political and

---

[1] «Estudio preliminar» to Florit's *Antología penúltima* (Madrid, 1970), p. 17.
[2] JOSÉ OLIVIO JIMÉNEZ asks whether Florit's latest poetry might have been composed partly as a reaction to the endeavors of the younger Cuban poets: «¿O quiso dar de paso, y por añadidura, con esta poesía sencilla y desaliñada, pero plena de humanidad y de vida, una lección que él podía considerar oportuna ante aquel otro empeño de ascendencia metafísica, pero de total hermetismo que la más joven generación cubana de entonces practicaba?» *Antología penúltima*, p. 23.

intellectual environment of the two decades before the advent of the Cuban Revolution, and the Revolution itself.[3]

Looking back at the poem Juan Ramón identified as the centerpiece of *Doble acento* (1937), «El martirio de San Sebastián», one can detect in the eagerness of the martyr an active will choosing to surrender unto death.

> Sí, venid a mis brazos, palomitas de hierro;
> palomitas de hierro, a mi vientre desnudo.
> (..)
> Sí, para que tengáis nido de carne
> y semillas de huesos ateridos;
> (..)
> Señor, ya voy por cauce de saetas.
> Sólo una más, y quedaré dormido.
> (..)
> Qué poco falta ya, Señor, para mirarte.
> Y miraré con ojos que vencieron las flechas;
> y escucharé tu voz con oídos eternos;
> y al olor de tus rosas me estaré como en éxtasis;
> (..)
> Ya voy, Señor. ¡Ay! qué sueño de soles,
> qué camino de estrellas en mi sueño.
> Ya sé que llega mi última paloma...
> ¡Ay! ¡Ya está bien, Señor, que te la llevo
> hundida en un rincón de las entrañas!

> *(AP,* pp. 91-92)

This exuberantly voiced acceptance, empowered by a vision of higher roads —another *campus stellae*— and richer options beyond death, could be taken as an affirmation at least correlative to the regenerative motions discussed in previous sections. Here the protagonist is still a struggler against a present pain that promises, and the promise still operates as a source of dignity and strength, rather than as an achieved reward.

In Florit's subsequent poetry, however, the peaceful sleep, the rosy ecstasies promised or expected as a reward for the willing toleration of present suffering, actually become the subject of the poetry. In a poem entitled «Al unicornio», and dated 1939, the surrender unto death no longer represents a forceful active struggle empowered by the faith in a fuller *sobre-vivencia,* but rather an escape to a flowery and lunar eternal meadow:

> (..)
> mira el desmayo, la quietud, la nada...

---

[3] Florit's disaffection for the Cuban Revolution was publicly expressed in no uncertain terms as early as 1962 in his speech «Sobre la Revolución cubana», delivered at Barnard College and reprinted in his *Obras completas,* 3 vols (Lincoln, Neb., 1982), III, pp. 319-25.

¿Nada?... Sobre la flor, bajo la tarde,
en las colinas del espíritu,
pace feliz el ser sacrificado
(...)

¿Nada?... Todo el camino de la muerte
por una eternidad de flor y luna.

(*AP*, p. 143)

Florit's tendency to uphold his static vision of life-after-death,[4] leads him away from the previously discussed stance of the strong creature evidenced in «Canción pequeñita» of *Doble acento,* where a desperate but empowered *agonista* expands the possibilities of his being by pursuing and expelling from the heart his deadening lack of courage. This renunciation of the efficacy of a creature's efforts develops, accompanied by an increasing reliance on the power of God as supplier of the requisite grace and blessedness. In this connection, it is interesting to juxtapose the 1942 rendition of the martyrdom of San Sebastián, against the original version of the early Thirties:

Flechado aquí, Señor, por tu belleza,
atado en aire al árbol del poniente
mira tu ardor y el alma de tu fuego.
Hombre, Señor, frente a la luz
que en hondos rayos atraviesa el alma;
un hombre sin destino, hoja en el viento
de ayer, besado por marchitas ondas
—aliento seco de la tierra muerta,
hoja de yerba en el impuro aliento
que sube, y llega, y al llegar ahoga,
y si quiere volar se amarra al suelo,
y cae, de cansado, en el abismo—,
un hombre, por tu gracia
aquí, Señor, te mira estremecido.

(*AP*, p. 220)

The emphasis in the first rendition of «Martirio...» highlights the will to ask for the sacrifice in terms that turn the flesh and bones of the martyr into the «nido» and «semillas» of his transcendence towards freedom. Conversely, the focus of «El nuevo San Sebastián» stresses the inefficacy of a creature who, despite his desire to fly upwards, falls defeated by his own inescapable ties to the ground. The sacrifice in the first «Martirio...» could be regarded as the fitting consummation in death of a life of efforts exerted to approach the God for whom the martyr dies. The sacrifice in the second version, however —the end of the life of an «hombre sin destino»—, does not consummate any pro-

---

[4] For other examples of Florit's vision of life-after-death, see «Momento de cielo» (*AP*, pp. 177-78), and «El tesoro» (*Antología poética* [México, 1956], p. 132).

gression or ascension of the living unto anything, and as such it represents a mere change of status accomplished by the grace of an external entity; it represents a mere escape from the limiting realm of the living to the pleasant pastures of the blessed dead. Finally, the ambivalent description of the state of the dead man as «Flechado» assigns to the recipient of God's agency a perpetuated passivity and uncomfortable immobility, distinct from the more active possibilities of the martyr in the earlier poem, who can at least fly by his «cauce de saetas», or by that «camino de estrellas de mi sueño».

Alongside Florit's increased dependence on his high regard for fixed states of harmony, serenity, or blessedness, there is another part of his poetic impulse which increasingly concentrates on detailed descriptions of the limitations of existence. This tendency, particularly pronounced in his collection «*Asonante final*» *y otros poemas* (1946-1955),[5] needs to be explored as yet another departure from the directions of Jiménez, Lezama and Vitier.

The poem that gives its name to the collection, «Asonante final» (1948), stands as the extreme example of Florit's unkempt poetry of the 40s, 50s and 60s. It could be argued that its length, its stream-of-consciousness formlessness, and its aim to be an autobiography of the spirit are reminiscent of Juan Ramón's «Espacio»,[6] but the colloquial —almost throw-away— nature of many of its untidy lines remains very much a feature all its own.

«Asonante final», intentionally or unintentionally, shows the work of a poet no longer in control of his poetry; just as it shows, intentionally or unintentionally, an individual who cannot sustain his efforts to affirm himself against the surrounding threats. The poem opens with a tortuous attempt to say something poetic which flounders on an embarrasingly self-conscious admission that the poet has lost the continuity of his assonant rhyme:

> Es tan difícil, tan terrible
> como pintar un árbol junto al río.
> Pero aun así voy a intentarlo
> (..)
> Y es que las horas y los días nos engañan,
> y nos dicen que hay tiempo, muchos años
> por delante, y nosotros creemos
> y esperamos...
> Pero no, hay que decirlo ahora,
> hay que cantar cuando aún hay canto,
> (..)

---

[5] First published by the *Orígenes* press in 1956.
[6] First published in México in 1943; *Cuadernos Americanos*, 2, no. 5, pp. 191-205.

Como se empieza a hablar y se balbuce,
como se empieza a andar y se tropieza,
como se empieza a ver y no se mira,
como se empieza a amar y no se sabe,
y se empieza a morir y no se siente;
como, en fin, ahora estoy escribiendo
estas palabras sin saber adonde
se han de clavar si se las lleva el viento;
como se me ha perdido el asonante
que había sido en ao
y ya no sé como será
porque todo está confuso y rápido
en la mente de Dios, que parece dormir
en esta tarde al otro lado
de su cielo de azules imposibles (...)

(*AP*, pp. 266-67)

Poetry here fulfils the function of recording the disorderly unraveling of an unfulfilled fate, precisely the opposite of manifesting «el Destino de una conciencia que se realiza» (*Leyenda*, 616). The speaker in the poem complains as he feels trapped between deceptive time and God's apparent lack of concern. He intends to sing despite the fact that the content of his song is merely the catalogue of his basic frustrations. The act of the poet here has very little to do with Lezama's ambition to «dissolve myrrh in the circumstantiality of the blood»; in fact, the poet intends to declare precisely how the circumstantiality of existence has frustrated every one of his efforts. He regards the efforts of learning to talk, to walk, to see, and to love as necessarily truncated. This stunted growth could be regarded as yet another way of voicing the aimless vacuity of the life of «un hombre sin destino».[7] Overtaken by all these frustrations, this individual represents a total failure with respect to Juan Ramón's imperatives to grow into a more attentive seeker, a more meaningful sayer, and consequently into a more nimble saver of those essences threatened by deceptive time —or even God's unconcern.

After a nostalgic catalogue of great authors read, and memories lived out, the poet concentrates his attention on the issue of death:

Digo que todo eso del olvido
y del acabar o del pasar
a mí me tiene sin cuidado.
Va uno por la calle preocupado
con una idea tonta, o vaya usted a saber,
tal vez alguna idea luminosa,
y de pronto, como el estornudar o el toser,
nos mata un automóvil y a otra cosa.

(*AP*, p. 271)

---

[7] «El nuevo San Sebastián» (*AP*, p. 220); quoted above.

If in the first Sebastián poem of the 30s death was a fitting consummation for a life totally sacrified to God, if in the second Sebastián rendition of 1942 death was a means of escape to static blessedness, here, in this autobiographical record of spiritual development up to 1948, death has been reduced to the subject of a flippant observation about an arbitrary inconvenience.[8]

At the end of the poem death is treated more seriously, but even so the fact of dying is not thereby heightened in value:

> ese día, aquel día
> en que me quede sordo de verdad,
> sordo absoluto, ya definitivo,
> y me estén llamando,
> llamando,
> llamando
> por todas las esquinas de mi cuerpo,
> sobre las páginas de mis libros,
> entre todas las letras de mis versos,
> y no contestaré, ¿qué habré de contestar?
> porque ya de una vez y para siempre
> me habré quedado muerto.
>
> (AP, pp. 278)

This closing endows death with a grim finality which essentially jars against much of what we have seen in previous sections —and against much of what we will continue to say— about Jiménez's, Lezama's and Vitier's views on death and resurrection.

Finally, I have to mention, at least, the title and the last poem of one of Florit's latest books —Hábito de esperanza (1936-1964). Sadly, what he hopes for amounts to just enough strength, not to overcome, but merely to tolerate the limitations of the given, which in his case do not quite rise to the pitch of great suffering or privation. Beyond that he seems to be resigned to a death which is merely the sad terminus of a life that is not regarded as the full deployment of some destiny. And if he has any hope of a life-after-death, it seems to be infused with conventional expectations of static blessedness —not at all related to the everyday habits of spiritual regeneration of the living. Hábito de esperanza ends with the following meditation on its epigraph by Francisco de Aldana, «Yo soy un hombre desvalido y solo»:

> Cuando me vaya, ¿qué? Los pocos versos
> que fui escribiendo al paso de la vida.
> Y nada más. Un árbol. Y sin hijos
> ni mujer. Será lo poco que deje.
> (................................)

---

[8] For another death poem which further documents this «progression» see «La muerte en el sol» (AP, p. 222).

¿Es lo bastante? Acaso sí lo sea
por lo que fui —pobre hombre solo,
triste de soledad cuando anochece—
Mas a pesar de todo agradecido
por lo que Dios me da de pan y lecho,
de amistad y familia. No me quejo...
Sólo que hubiera sido tan alegre
eso de ver el mundo de la mano
del buen amor que no ha querido ser...
Y no será jamás. Ya *nevermore*.
Que el aire del invierno me rodea
para purificarme de mis sueños
y así dejarme a lo que soy: un hombre
solo y por desvalido, un alma seca
al amor de la lumbre que se apaga,
siempre esperando lo que nunca llega.

(*AP*, p. 342)

This poem is successful only insofar as the self-pity of the speaker enlists the reader's compassion. Yet the record of the sadness, the lonesomeness, and the resignation is not in line with the demands of taking on a «camino mundo arriba», nor is reality infused with the required «Destino de una conciencia que la realiza». Florit's «hábito de esperanza» becomes a habit of waiting passively for the end of a limited and devalued existence, rather than a habit of hoping through which the hopes are given substance by the efforts of an active hand. If this is the extent of «su verdad», the obligation to live by it would not take him, or anyone, very far in the daily business of growing and overcoming.

VIII

LEZAMA AFTER 1939: «LA SUSTANCIA DE LO INEXISTENTE»

How far do Lezama and Vitier take the development of their *conciencia*? What comes to represent for them the highest actualization of their respective *destinos*?

The work of both authors, in different degrees, provide these two questions with the same two answers: Resurrection and Revolution. Lezama will refer to the promises of the Cuban Revolution as the new historical context in which a whole country will manifest his personal normative ambition of always attempting the impossible, but most of all, he will dedicate a significant part of his work to the exploration of how poetry and poetics seek, express and demand the actualization of the most distant and scandalous of all impossibilities —the Resurrection. Vitier, on the other hand, will refer to the wide vistas afforded by a faithful pursuit of the Resurrection, but most of all, he will dedicate a much more significant part of his career to the critical perpetuation of the revitalising promises of the Cuban Revolution.

Any reader of Lezama will soon realise that my present discussion of the Resurrection as a theme in his work is intended to be merely introductory rather than exhaustive. The limited scope of the present study requires that the presentation of the issues be subordinated to their confluence or related divergence with regard to the discussed contributions of Juan Ramón and the other two Cuban poets. In order to achieve this specific level of consonance I have deliberately avoided any reference to Lezama's exceedingly demanding poetry, as well as any reference to the complications of Lezama's critical vocabulary.

The very center of Lezama's *Paradiso*[1] describes the message of José Cemí's mother, Rialta, to the young man after his participation in the student demonstrations of 1930 against the Machado dictatorship:

[1] Pages 320-22 of a novel that starts on page 4 and ends on page 645 (México, 1975).

69

> Mientras esperaba tu regreso, pensaba en tu padre y en ti, rezaba el rosario
> y me decía: ¿Qué le diré a mi hijo cuando regrese de ese peligro? El paso
> de cada cuenta del rosario, era el ruego de que una voluntad te acompañara
> a lo largo de la vida, que siguieses un punto, una palabra, que tuvieses siem-
> pre una obsesión que te llevase siempre a buscar lo que se manifiesta y lo
> que se oculta. Una obsesión que nunca destruyese las cosas, que buscase
> en lo manifestado lo oculto, en lo secreto lo que asciende para que la luz
> lo configure. (...) Oyeme lo que te voy a decir: No rehúses el peligro, pero
> intenta siempre lo más difícil.[2]

In his introduction to Lezama's *Obras,* Vitier himself[3] discusses this
passage, and the subsequent description of the son's response to the
mother's advice for which the narrator adopts the first person singular
for the only time in the novel:

> Sé que esas son las palabras más hermosas que Cemí oyó en su vida, después
> de las que leyó en los Evangelios, y que nunca oirá otras que lo pongan tan
> decididamente en marcha.[4]

«Ponerse en marcha hacia lo más difícil», should stand as an illuminating
correlative to Juan Ramón's demand of «emprender mi camino mundo
arriba».

Lezama bases his insistence on the need to develop beyond the possible on the premise that real progress involves, not a successive harnessing of knowledge for the sake of accurate prediction and pragmatic control of reality, but rather a spiralling creative process that brings into
being what has been so far envisioned as inexistent. The demand to
attempt the impossible is supplemented by Saint Paul's radically innova-
tive definition of faith in Hebrews 11:1. Lezama paraphrases and elaborates:

> La sustancia de lo inexistente, la vieja y no superada definición de la fe
> sigue sosteniendo y apoyando, soplando y arrasando. (...) Lo inexistente no
> sólo tiene una gravitación, sino una forma, inclusive una sustancia, una
> superación del mundo griego y sensorial, lo inexistente, es el desarrollo, sin
> metamorfosis, por la fe.[5]

The concept of «desarrollo por la fe» can be seen as related to Juan
Ramón's project of development of an individual consciousness to ma-
turity, creativity, or even to the extreme indentification of the creature
with divinity. This elaboration on the Pauline definition of faith, can
also be seen as related to developmental processes beyond the sphere of
the individual. For instance, much of the relevance and appeal of contemporary Liberation Theology depends precisely on the opposition of

---

2 *Paradiso (Obras completas,* vol. I), p. 321.
3 VITIER, «Introducción a la obra de José Lezama Lima», I, p. lvi.
4 *Paradiso,* p. 322.
5 LEZAMA, «La dignidad de la poesía», II, p. 771.

the possibilities afforded by this «desarrollo por la fe» against the imposition of a materialist «desarrollo» by the acquisition and control of products and currency. This development by faith through which the creature
voices and creates the previously non-existent raises the creature to the
status of creator, not only in the individual sense of developing an individual *conciencia*, but also in the more global sense of developing his
social and political ethos.

The Greek term *poiesis*, insofar as it means «making»», «forming»,
«creating» as well as «poetry», has always attracted Lezama's interest,[6]
and grafting the coincidence of all those meanings in that one word on
to the Pauline assertion about faith, Lezama postulates the poet as the
guardian of the substance of the inexistent.[7] Basing himself on such a
postulate, he can go on to say:

> Al llegar el poeta a constituirse en guardián del inexistente sustantivo, la
> poesía tenía que gravitar como el testimonio de la sentencia que iba a ceñir
> la nueva sustancia.[8]

This bringing into being of what does not exist seems to be one step
removed from Juan Ramón's exercises of *poiesis*, which —in comparison— seem «limited» to realising what is already pre-existent *in potentia*,
and to creating new entities from already-created elements. Lezama
suggests that when the poet's words fall or are placed in new arrangements —concepts, metaphors, images— at that very moment the inexistent is named and begins to be. The «sentencia» gives witness, *da fe de,
da fe a*, the new substance already «ceñida» by the poetry. For Lezama,
poetry continues the work which Poetry/Logos started In The Beginning.

According to Lezama, the Resurrection is one of those images which
already has been voiced, and as voiced it is already exerting its gravitation beyond the challenge it represents to logical and rationalistic understanding. Furthermore, since it stands as the most challenging, the
most absurd of all images, Lezama insists that its substantivation should
be pursued with special zeal.

The basic differences between Resurrection, immortality, and eternal
life have to be discussed, even if cursorily. While the idea of «immortality» postulates that the soul does not die despite the observable decay
and destruction of the body, and while the concept of «eternal life» pre-
sumes an extension of the present conditions of the living ignoring or
trivialising the fact of death, a serious conception of the Resurrection
proposes the validity of a radical contradiction that acknowledges the
irreversible finality of death, and upholds the possibility of a complete
restitution of the full person —body, soul and processes— beyond death.

---

[6] «La dignidad de la poesía» opens with a discussion of *poiesis;* II, p. 761.
[7] *Obras completas*, II, p. 774.
[8] *Obras completas*, II, p. 775.

The Resurrection also has to be differentiated from all those poetically or epiphanically induced regenerative processes discussed in previous sections. While the progressive, regenerative exercises of «cultivo» and «conciencia» towards a «destino» oppose chaos-producing entropy and deadening inertia, the Resurrection stands as a repossession of life after the final and total energetic collapse. If the previously discussed resuscitations revitalise, or re-energise, the Resurrection re-creates in the fullest extent of the word, and as such it is the ultimate act of *poeisis*.

It is difficult, and perhaps unnecessary, to discuss the extent to which Lezama managed to give substance to the full demands beyond the absurdity of the Resurrection. But it is important to realise the extent to which his pursuit of the impossible was essential to all his «marchas mundo arriba». *Paradiso* is the impossible novel and the impossible poem. And his observations in «Las eras imaginarias» amount to the poetic re-evaluation of those periods of history in which an image —the impossible voiced, and demanding its full manifestation— becomes the ordering principle of a social contract. Among his «Eras imaginarias» he discusses the theocratic synthesis of the Egyptians for whom the image of the life of the dead permeated all social and cultural manifestations, and all those periods in which the king stands as a symbol of the presence of divine authority from Caesar and Charlemagne to the canonised medieval monarchs. Finally, he proposes the possibility of a contemporary «Era imaginaria» in the following prophetic terms:

> La última era imaginaria a la cual voy a aludir en esta ocasión, es la posibilidad infinita, que entre nosotros la acompaña José Martí. Entre las mejores cosas de la Revolución cubana, reaccionando contra la era de la locura que fue la etapa de la disipación, de la falsa riqueza, está el haber traído de nuevo el espíritu de la pobreza irradiante, del pobre sobre abundante por los dones del espíritu. (...)
>
> La Revolución cubana significa que todos los conjuros negativos han sido decapitados. (...) Comenzamos a vivir nuestros hechizos y el reinado de la imagen se entreabre en un tiempo absoluto. Cuando el pueblo está habitado por una imagen viviente, el estado alcanza su figura.[9]

In the following discussion on Vitier this passage will be briefly reconsidered in an account of Juan Ramón's ethical, political and poetical ideal of his «inmensa minoría» —the non-materialistic aristocracy of the spirit. Lezama's tribute to the Cuban Revoluttion is presented as evidence of what he regarded as the capacity of poetry to infuse even history —global *destino*— with the power of the image to bring the impossible into being, to actualise «mundo arriba» «el desarrollo por la fe».

---

[9] «A partir de la poesía» (1960), *Obras completas*, II, pp. 838-39.

IX

VITIER AFTER 1939: «DE LA ... POESIA
A LA ... CONCIENCIA»

After the initial awe of the fifteen-year-old apprentice before the master, and after his subsequent distancing from specifically Juanramonian directions, Cintio Vitier comes to acknowledge a renewed interest in the work and thought of Juan Ramón Jiménez in the following terms:

> Su influencia en mí, después del vuelco vallejiano que pareció situarme en las antípodas, se siguió ejerciendo más profundamente a través de su poesía americana, desde *Animal de fondo* hasta «Espacio», con un hambre de realidad que a la postre se sumó en mí a la del peruano, hambre cifrada en este verso clave para mi deseo. «El más, el más, camino único de la sabiduría».[1]

A hunger for reality leads Vitier in his earliest poetry through the involved hermetic explorations of memories, desires and ontological uncertainty. These fifteen years of poetic practice included in *Vísperas* (1938-1953) chart very carefully the development of a consciousness intent on looking inwards and backwards to the roots of the present manifestations of his being; as such, *Vísperas* represents a relentless search for *orígenes,* and towards knowledge of the self in relationship to the darkest constituents of reality. It would be possible to relate this form of «¡Cavar!» to some of the motions already discussed as particularly Juanramonian. But since in the case of Vitier they could be regarded as much more confluent with the work of other poets like Lezama and Vallejo, I shall leave *Vísperas* after a brief discussion of the way in which this book stands as a preparation for the discoveries of *Testimonios* (1953-1968), where Juan Ramón's imperatives of developing *conciencia* towards *destino* find an auspicious context in the challenges of the Cuban Revolution.

Vitier's project of self-knowledge as charted in *Vísperas* could be regarded as his pilgrimage towards a threshold where the man who knows himself stands inquisitive and attentive, but not accomplishing very

---

[1] «El momento cubano de Juan Ramón Jiménez», p. 9. col. 4. The line by Juan Ramón comes from «En mi mar tercero», *Animal de fondo* (*LP*, p. 1296).

much beyond the repeated formulation in words —not acts— of what is felt as beckoning beyond the threshold:

> Los pasos pueden llevarnos a algunos lugares, lo cual no significa nada (por el momento); a otros sitios nacemos o advenimos sin pasos discernibles, con pasos tan borrados que el testimonio puede salir como una llamarada incontenible, aguda o sorda. Más nocturna maravilla es que nos sintamos comparecer ante nosotros mismos.
> Cuando ocurre lo segundo, el cuerpo adquiere su verdadera forma interrogante, la forma de su placer o de su angustia, y se distiende para lanzar la flecha que le piden. (...) El desconcierto de nuestra ambición es sólo respondido por la pregunta que nos salta de la entraña (mi pregunta eterna): ¿y esto? ¿Y esto que me conmueve? ¿Y yo qué voy a hacer *con esto*?
> Nada es más importante: ni hay pregunta más parecida a un hogar.
> (*Vísperas*, p. 110)

At this juncture, the speaker of this poem, written between 1945 and 1946, does not possess any more answers to his perennial question than the speaker of the previously quoted poem «Humo» from «Luz ya sueño» (1938-1942). But in this case a new question becomes the answer to his confused ambition, and a residence, «un hogar», from which one could project oneself as the «flecha» one is required to become. The impulse to know more about oneself, the guiding principle of *Vísperas*, has placed the knower and the known face to face, and as self-knowledge judges the self it knows, the verdict becomes the imperative to take the discovered self as the «*esto*» with which something has to be done, accomplished, realised.

In an essay dated 1945-1947 Vitier himself explains the way in which thresholds represent unavoidable imperatives: «Todo umbral significa una responsabilidad sagrada, el comienzo de una nueva dirección universal. Revela y compromete, juzga y obliga a tomar partido en el universo, a escoger definitivamente».[2] If *Vísperas* represents that initial stage in the development of a *conciencia* towards a threshold, *Testimonios* amounts to the record of the choices of that *conciencia* as it precipitates itself —vocationally or otherwise— beyond the threshold and towards its *destino*.

The first section of *Testimonio*, «Canto llano» (1953-1955),[3] elaborates, most of all, the painful reluctance of an individual who heeds the demands to move «mundo arriba» or «to attempt always the impossible», and yet cannot will the impetus or grace to act in accord with those

---

[2] «Mnemosyne», *Poética* (Madrid, 1973), p. 10.
[3] First published in book form as *Canto llano* by the *Orígenes* press in 1956, it is generally regarded as Vitier's most significant poetic contribution. Part of its general acclaim depends on its accessibility when compared with Vitier's previous poetry, and on its avoidance of that more explicitly political commitment of the voice developed in subsequent books.

demands which already loom over him solidly and ultimately validated and compelling.

The first of the fifty short and metrically manicured «plain songs» states the following:

> ¿Quién eres que así me exiges
> lo que no está en mi poder?
> Déjame, oscuro, gozar
> la pobreza de mi ser.
>
> (*Testimonios*, p. 11)

The speaker recognises and resents the demands to grow and make more of himself. But alongside his feeling that the imperative might tyrannise him by forcing him to take up a path of development quite unrelated to what he thinks he is, the recognition of his condition as one of «pobreza de mi ser» could very well become the necessary point of departure towards the enrichment of his poor being.

The second «canto llano» takes the confrontation with these demands further:

> (...................................)
> Era una orden silenciosa
> que no podía yo cumplir.
>
> (...................................)
> Era una súplica muy débil
> que no quería discernir.
>
> Hasta que el *no* llenó mi casa,
> mis árboles y mi vivir
> y empecé a ver que amanecía
> la blancura de consentir.
>
> (*Testimonios*, p. 12)

Saying «No» to the demands felt, and, most importantly, hearing oneself voicing the negation, amounts to a recognition of the reluctance, of the barriers that do not allow the self to yield to the imperatives at hand. As we say «No, not That», our stance indicates that we have at least «discerned» something of what «That» entails. After this kind of an encounter with the demands —negative, but clearly negative and therefore real— the reader starts moving towards that «consentir» demanded by the «orden silenciosa» and the «súplica muy débil». As the adjectives associated with the imperatives are not imperious at all, this gentleness does much to dispel the potential tyranny of the demands. Finally, the four hyming infinitives «cumplir», «discernir», «vivir», «consentir», invite us to explore their relationship as they conspire against our indolence.

Even if the two «plain songs» discussed seem to point to openings beyond the present reluctance to surrender to the demands of growing, there are poems in this section which emphasise the possibility of completely failing to respond to any positive callings beyond the thresholds, or the possibility of responding to options that will make deformed monsters out of those who respond:

> Quema, hiende, rompe
> la ciudad humana
> y dibuja lo invisible
> formas extrañas.
>
> (.................................)
>
> Salvaje erosión de oscura
> piedra humanada,
> y por dentro pasando
> las hieles bárbaras.
>
> Se nos va hinchando la vida,
> deforma su ala,
> para acabar sepultando
> monstruos de nada.
>
> *(Testimonios, p. 36)*

Other poems suggest radical ways of opposing this external imposition that originates in the dehumanising City of Man and leads to the monstrosity and the nothingness:

> Restitúyase el agua al agua,
> el aire al aire, el fuego al fuego
> y sobre todo al barro
> el arrogante cuerpo.
>
> Devuélvete, ladrón del ser
> y de la nada despensero,
> que lo usurpado altera
> el orden justiciero.
>
> (.................................)
>
> Desposeyéndote, serás
> el espejo del universo,
> lavada al fin la culpa
> de haber alzado un sueño.
>
> *(Testimonios, p. 39)*

Juan Ramón, in his prologue of 1937 to Florit's *Doble acento,* had insisted on an «acto de poderío inmanente, en que nuestro ser llega, por intensidad de contemplación, a darse cuenta de su elemento, a entenderse, como otro elemento, con los elementos».[4] Vitier voices a similar imperative in which the state of elemental harmony is achieved after a revitalising rejection of everything that does not truly belong to the

---

[4] *La corriente infinita,* p. 148; quoted above.

self. The weak object pronoun as a suffix to the imperative verb «devuél-vete» creates an ambiguity which can be glossed either as «give yourself back», or no less suggestively, as «give yourself back to yourself». This process of self-devolution can be seen as specifically applicable to all those material ties which hold one fast to «la ciudad humana» of the previous poem. Giving ourselves back to ourselves, and to an arrangement of reality in which acquisitions of Being do not tamper with the just order of things is equivalent to a rejection of all investments in that Human City which breeds monstrosity and nothingness in and out of us.

Te tensions between the opening afforded by the demands to grow, and the difficulties or obstacles that inhibit the possibilities of growth, are resolved only partially in «Canto llano». Those poems that uphold the openings to the positive possibilities set the overall tone of the section, but this positivity is supported, most of all, by its numerous imperative statements. So many imperatives in some sense express the intent of the speaker to act in accordance with them, yet in another sense they show a *conciencia* which has stepped over the threshold of commitment far enough to voice the directives of its *destino,* but not far enough to speak of its achievements against indeterminacy and evil in the more assured and reliable indicative mood.

Another set of tensions issue from the way the collection does not clarify whether the options beyond the imperatives operate in a specifically political and ethical sphere, or in a specifically religious and metaphysical one. «La ciudad humana» could be a cipher for the corrupt world in the ethical-political sense of an unjust order, or in the religious-metaphysical sense of an ungodly pit of non-being. Furthermore, the cleansing act of self-dispossession could be regarded as the requisite for an ethically and politically sound redistribution of material wealth, or as a religious and metaphysical redefinition of the self as purged and regenerated.

The lack of clarification on this account is more enlightening than confusing. Even if «Canto llano» presents a *conciencia* not yet accomplished in the actualization of what is recognised as its potential, the book already points to ways of regeneration and fulfilment in which religious, metaphysical, political and ethical concerns appear equivocally evoked by the same images.

In «Escrito y cantado» (1954-1959) Vitier's language and imagery continues to develop that simultaneous political and religious referentiality, but in the context of a successive deterioration of whatever loud affirmation might have been derived from the resonant imperatives of «Canto llano». The way out from the depths of the final stages of this lapse into despair is found only through a full confrontation with the violence and the revelations afforded by the events that ushered in the triumph of the Cuban Revolution in January 1959.

77

The regression can be documented with a few fragments, starting with an excerpt from the first poem of the collection:

> Ciertamente
> hay crimen, hay miseria, un espanto
> insondable se agiganta desde el principio,
> y algunos alcanzan la contemplación o la obediencia
> en sus diversos grados.
>
> Toda abominación y toda gloria
> en cierto modo atañen.
>
> (*Testimonios*, p. 67)

The speaker adopts a prophetic tone to talk about the increment of evil, which could be either cosmic evil and general sinfulness, just as it could be specific social corruption. The mention of the few that seem to be coping with the inevitability of all that evil or corruption could refer to the religious contemplative, or to any kind of disciplined individual committed to exerting his efforts against all that negativity in any sphere of activity. But it is not clear whether this mention is intended as an encouraging assurance that at least some people exert themselves against the abominations, or as a discouraging reminder that they are very few. Finally, the words «abominación» and «gloria», despite their tendency to be associated with specifically religious vocabulary, can now be seen as equally applicable to the more secular sphere of politics and ethics.

The difficulties or obstacles encountered by the individual on his way towards the fulfilment of the ontological imperatives appear as completely paralysing in the following poem:

> Parada en seco, atroz, la criatura
> en vano busca el ser de su quimera.
> «No puedo más», exclama, y ni siquiera
> siente el sabor feliz de la amargura.
>
> (*Testimonios*, p. 85)

This paralysis which more and more closes all the openings envisioned in «Canto llano» finally arrives at the commonplace equation of the lifeless motions of the living with Hell. In this Hell existence amounts to a farcical imitation of hopes, rather than a directed development towards what Lezama and Saint Paul would call «the assurance of things hoped for»:

> Estaba condenado
> a sostener el simulacro de la vida
> pues yo también imitaba mi esperanza.
> (...)
> Entonces comprendí que era el infierno.
>
> (*Testimonios*, p. 86)

Since Vitier entitled this poem «El apócrifo», we can infer that this kind of vision of life as hell has been voiced against that most inauthentic part of him which at this moment has completely overwhelmed the more vital manifestations of his being.

The last five poems of the collection, clearly differentiated from the others, display their dates of composition from the last months of 1958 to the first months of 1959, and identify the coming of the Cuban Revolution as the way out from the hell penetrated during the lapse of «Escrito y cantado». Thus the *Testimonios* of Cintio Vitier record the continuation of the project of growth envisioned in «Canto llano» as his spiritual development merges with, and depends upon, the liberating deployment of historical events.

«Agonía» —the long prose poem dated a month or so before the final collapse of the Batista regime— describes the experience of listening to the sniping in La Habana as the preamble to the speaker's spiritual odyssey. His reflections carry him from the false sense of communion with the urban guerrilleros, to the subsequent infernal vision of the suffering in the torture chambers of the city, and all the way down to a point of total despair at which the *agonista* confesses to have lost even his capacity to turn his agony into that rock-bottom certitude that things can get no worse, to a point at which his pain does not even assure him of the reality of his suffering self. The poem ends as follows:

> Las detonaciones casi eran, en el frescor nocturno, un alivio, un consuelo. Pero tenía que ver los rostros bestiales (...) Ver la sangre, y, sobre todo, lo que más atravesaba mis entrañas, ver la esperanza que no ceja en el torturado ni en el torturador (...) La esperanza reducida al último escondrijo, allí latiendo como alimaña acorralada. Las detonaciones se confundían con el alba, (...) con las voces que venían a verificar el mundo (...); un mundo lleno de injusticia. (...) y entonces comprendí que se alejaba de mi alma, con las sombras, el único don en que podíamos confiar: el poder de la agonía.
>
> XI-1958   *(Testimonios*, pp. 115-16)

The acknowledgement of the degradation of hope leads to a secular restatement of Christ's «¡Dios mío, por qué me has abandonado!» expressed in terms of the loss of the sufferer's capacity to turn despair into power of being.

If «Agonía» registers the voice of someone utterly overwhelmed by the horrors of a pre-revolutionary reality ridden by pain, injustice and «rostros bestiales», «El rostro» registers the voice of someone who finds in the countenance of the peasant guerrillero the liberating presence of a saviour, and the compelling human exemplar capable of satiating the seeker's ever-present hunger for truth:

79

Te he buscado sin tregua, toda mi vida te he buscado, y cada vez te enmascarabas más y dejabas que pusieran en tu sitio un mascarón grotesco, imagen del deshonor y del vacío.

Y te volvías un enigma de locura, un jeroglífico banal, y ya no sabíamos quiénes éramos, dónde estábamos, cuál era el sabor de los alimentos del cuerpo y del espíritu.

¡Pero hoy, al fin, te he visto, rostro de mi patria! Y ha sido tan sencillo como abrir los ojos.

Sé que de pronto la visión va a cesar, que ya se está desvaneciendo, que la costumbre amenaza invadirlo todo otra vez con sus vastas oleadas. Por eso me apresuro a decir:

El rostro vivo, mortal y eterno de mi patria está, en el rostro de esos hombres humildes que han venido a libertarnos.

Yo los miro como quien bebe y come lo único que puede saciarlo. Yo los miro para llenar mi alma de verdad. Porque ellos son la verdad.

Porque en estos campesinos, y no en ningún libro ni poemas ni paisajes ni conciencia ni memoria se verifica la sustancia de la patria como en el día de su resurrección.

6-I-1959   (*Testimonios*, pp. 120-21)

The poem displays all the symptoms of a classic conversion experience: life-long quest achieved, spiritual starvation satiated, truth envisioned as incarnated and accessible. It is important to note, however, that despite the enthusiasm of the new convert, Vitier qualifies his urgency to sing the contents of his revelation introducing the sharp critical insight about his sad certainty that if he waits, the deteriorating tendencies within reality will defuse and destroy the fullness of the vision. Beyond this caveat, the specific mention of the resurrection at the end of the poem relates the entrance of the *Ejército Rebelde* in La Habana to the events celebrated on any Easter Sunday, the triumph of a saviour who through the drama of overcoming his agony unto death has been able to infuse the world with the fullness of life of a new creation. In retrospect, this mention of the resurrection forces us to recognise the quite unsubtle eucharistical and Christological baggage of «Agonía» as part of a re-enactment of Good Friday horrors.

As an important member of the Grupo de *Orígenes* Vitier was well versed in their shared tendencies to express metaphysical concerns in generally religious, somewhat heterodox, and specifically neo-scholastic terms. Furthermore, his use of images simultaneously charged with political, ethical, religious and metaphysical significance should not be regarded as surprising in an avowed admirer of the poetry of César Vallejo. What is interesting to point out in this respect is that Vitier's use of poetry as a record of imperatives for ontological development capable of being realised in either political or religious directions, *or both,* predates the present day insistence of Latin American Liberation Theologians and poets like Camilo Torres or Ernesto Cardenal on the need to foster both kinds of directions simultaneously. We can understand the way in which Liberation Theology stresses the relatedness between the political or ethical and the religious or metaphysical, by focusing on the term *liberation* as an equivocal pointer to the specifically political requirements of emancipation, as well as to the specifically religious quest for redemption. The same relatedness underlies the terms «resurrection» and «insurrection», both connected in the mind of the oppressed —much more than merely etymologically— with the motions of *raising.*

Another example of Vitier's explicit treatment of the interrelatedness of specifically Christian and revolutionary issues, can be found in his poem «Viernes Santo». In this poem Vitier sees the secular efforts of any labourer participating in the making of the Cuban Revolution as a practice of Christ's testimony, even if the practice lacks all reference to Jesus himself. At the same time, this poem presents Christ's acceptance of these labours as fully validated, because whatever the revolutionary workers get done with their work and their loving, the Saviour does not have to do.

> Y [estás] en el esfuerzo de los hombres
> de buena voluntad,
> inconscientes del tesoro
> que llevan a tu pecho
> del aire que te dan, del poco alivio
> que traen sus manos rudas, ciegas
> al horror de tu agonía
> que no acaba.
>
> (................................)
>
> En verdad te gustaría
> mientras mueres,
> que todo fuera muy bien hecho
> con alegría y con amor,
> y que la cena humeara feliz
> mientras bajas al sepulcro.
>
> (................................)
>
> Los que piensan en el prójimo
> y lo ayudan y trabajan para él
> son tus discípulos:
> no importa que lo ignoren.
>
> *(Testimonios,* pp. 279-80)

«Viernes Santo» is part of a collection written between 1967 and 1968 and compiled under the suggestive title of «Entrando en materia»: Getting to the heart of the matter, as well as actually getting immersed

81

in matter as such. The discipleship described in «Viernes Santo» is very much part of these spiritual activities, since it concentrates on the way in which a secular but just social order infuses material reality with those imperatives of love and work for others usually regarded as exclusively Christian. The poem suggests that as matter is transformed by work into those gifts of love that satisfy the needs of the people, the voluntary revolutionary worker participates in the kind of creative act by which the saviour infuses matter with the gifts of the spirit.

As we survey the continuation of Vitier's trajectory, already well within the new possibilities and challenges afforded by the Cuban Revolution, we can again refer to its qualified confluence with Juan Ramón's mystical, ethical and political formulations of his latest years. In «Viernes Santo» for instance, when Vitier says:

> El hombre y la naturaleza están absortos,
> entregados a sus relaciones
> de producción, de lucha y goce.
> No hay nada que purgar.
>
> (*Testimonios*, p. 278)

it is very difficult to disregard the echo of Juan Ramón's assertion in *Dios deseado y deseante*:

> Yo nada tengo que purgar.
> Toda mi impedimenta
> no es sino fundación para este hoy
> en que al fin te deseo (...)
>
> (*LP*, p. 1289)

Both poets negate the guilt of man as the basis for their relationship with the divine in terms which Vitier, an avid reader of *Animal de fondo*, must have recognised as specifically Juanramonian. Both poets uphold the capacity of humans to be involved in acts that fully relate them to reality in ways that give them access to a humanly earned state of blessedness, to a humanly accomplished participation in the prerogatives of the divine. The difference in the focus of the two poets also demands attention: for Juan Ramón freedom depends on an individual assertion of his developed *conciencia,* while for Vitier freedom depends on that individual's participation in acts of production, struggle and joy which have been made possible by the collective adoption of the post-revolution arrangement of reality in which, as Lezama says, «todos los conjuros negativos han sido decapitados».

In the first chapter of his book, *Juan Ramón Jiménez en Cuba,* Vitier acknowledges the impact of «El trabajo gustoso» (1936) and «Límite del progreso» (1937) from the perspective of a critic who sees many of the imperatives enunciated in both statements as fully manifested in the achievements and challenges of the Cuban Revolution[5]. The following excerpt from the very short piece «El hombre inmune» represents a poignant synthesis of Juan Ramón's concerns in the two longer essays which Vitier discusses.

> El comunismo capitalista, mina, tesoro, sostén de las actuales colmenas decadentes, con centro de parasitismo vicioso y alrededor de virtuosa esclavitud, ha de ceder al comunismo idealista, lírico subjetivo: comunismo comunista en lo necesario, lo suficiente material, e individualista en lo infinito inmaterial, espiritual; y no hay otro comunismo para el hombre mejor. (Entre los dos, quedará nulo, como un absurdo tránsito, el imposible comunismo totalitario, tan estéril, tan seco, tan yerto como las dictaduras de tipo fascista o nacista que son su propio revés o derecho, según quien mire.) El verdadero hombre, es decir, el trabajador verdadero, material o intelectual, no podrá nunca soportar dictaduras de castillo ni de plaza, cadena de oro ni de hierro, en lo vocativo.
>
> El hombre tristemente mecanizado, diente de los engranajes babilónicos, debe recobrar del progreso, con o contra el progreso y por su propia rueda, su lójico tamaño, su fuerza misma, su auténtica individualidad. Lo social no puede ser una enfermedad para el hombre, como es ahora, sino una inmunidad. Sin su aliento, su proporción, su libertad, nada puede, aunque parezca que puede mucho, el hombre.
>
> El estado normal, justo, efectivo del progreso jeneral es aquel en que todos seamos «aristócratas», digo, «sencillos seres de profundo cultivo interior»; aquel en cuya raya el hombre no parezca, no pueda parecer pequeño, cansado, ni preso.[6]

In «Viernes Santo» the worker who fulfills his Christian discipleship without reference to Christ is a good candidate for Juan Ramón's aristocracy of the spirit. Not only does he work and love, but he already lives within an economy in which the unavailability of unnecesary —and even necessary— consumer products, represents a new freedom from the exploitative limitations imposed by the dependence on the external sources of most of those products. Vitier's poem «Escasez», also from «Entrando en materia», describes this new freedom:

> Lo que no hay
> primero brilla como una estrella altiva,
> después se va apagando
> en el espacio vacío, consolador y puro
> de lo que hay.
>
> Amanece.
>
> La ciudad está llena de su carencia
> como de una luz
> distinta.
>
> (*Testimonios*, p. 288)

---

[5] *Juan Ramón Jiménez en Cuba*, pp. 10-13, 23-25. Reprinted in *Sin Nombre*, 12, no. 3 (1982), pp. 36-39, 50-52.

[6] «El hombre inmune» (1937), *La corriente infinita*, p. 277.

This auspicious light of scarcity dawns on the same city described in «Agonía» some years earlier as the stage for another *amanecer* in a world «lleno de injusticia». The scarcity represents the achievement of Juan Ramón's rejection of the gadget-cluttered world, and the requisite for Lezama's «nuevo espíritu de la pobreza irradiante».

Finally, to return to the central issue of the role of poetry in all projects of developing *conciencia mundo arriba,* this section concludes with Vitier's «Cántico nuevo», where the subordination of poetry to the importance of everything else sounds like a denunciation of Juan Ramón's doctrines about the primacy of poetry, while, in fact, it represents the culmination of an apprenticeship that has taken the younger poet all the way to the transformation of the self through and beyond the leadings of his poetic métier.

> Este libro no es tanto de poesía
> como de conciencia.
>
> (..)
>
> La poesía no está por encima de nada.
>
> Echo mi vida a un fuego: ser honrado.
> Como no voy a querer serlo si en ello me va la vida.
> No la que otros pueden darme o quitarme
>   sino la que yo me doy
> en mi conciencia, que Dios me dio
> para hacer este cántico nuevo,
> áspero, duro, desabrido.
>
> He pasado de la conciencia de la poesía
> a la poesía de la conciencia.
>
>   **(Testimonios, p. 300)**

CONCLUSION

HABITS OF CREATION

Operative habit resides chiefly in the mind or the will... Habits are interior growths of spontaneous life... and only the living (that is to say, only minds which are perfectly alive) can acquire them, because they alone are capable of raising the level of their being by their own activity: they possess, in such an enrichment of their faculties, secondary motives to action, which they bring into play when they want... Such a habit is a virtue, that is to say, a quality which, triumphing over the original indetermination of the intellective faculty, at once sharpening and hardening the point of its activity, raises it in respect of a definite object to a maximum of perfection, and so of operative efficiency. Art is a virtue of the practical intellect.

(JACQUES MARITAIN, *Art and Scholasticism;* quoted by Sally Fitzgerald in *The Habit of Being: The Letters of Flannery O'Connor,* p. xv.)

In every encounter with reality the structures of the self and the world are interdependently present. The most fundamental expression of this fact is the language which gives man the power to abstract from the concretely given and, after having abstracted from it, to interpret and transform it. The most vital being is the being which has the word and by the word is liberated from bondage to the given. In every encounter with reality man is always beyond this encounter. He knows about it, he compares it, he is tempted by other possibilities, he anticipates the future as he remembers the past. This is his freedom, and in this freedom the power of his life consists. It is the source of his vitality.

(PAUL TILLICH, *The Courage to Be,* p. 82.)

The words of Jacques Maritain and Paul Tillich focus on the issue of habits and language in ways that help to recapitulate much of what I have proposed in this study. When Maritain defines habits as «interior growth of spontaneous life», he is referring to internal developments that allow us to reenact the fullness and freshness of enlivening miracles over and over again. He is referring to the kind of capacity which Lezama ascribed to Juan Ramón and Picasso —and demands of everyone— with the vivid metaphor of the skin-sloughing crystal serpent. When Maritain asserts that only minds that are perfectly alive can acquire these habits «because they alone are capable of raising the level of their being (...) to a maximum perfection», he is referring to what has been presented as Juan Ramón's imperative to develop *conciencia* towards *destino, mundo arriba;* and to what Vitier learned from Juan Ramón's exclamatory assertion in *Dios deseado y deseante,* «El más, el más, camino único de la sabiduría».

The role of language in the development of those habits becomes one of the most thoroughly-shared preoccupations of these and so many other poets. What Tillich points out about the centrality of language in all dealings with reality summarises a great number of the concerns elaborated by Juan Ramón, Lezama, Vitier, and to a lesser degree, by Florit. «The power to abstract from the concretely given» amounts to an Aristotelian reformulation of the more explicitly Platonic motion by which Juan Ramón delights in the revitalising discovery of the relationship between word, name, meaning and thing. Furthermore, Tillich's assertion that the power of language and language users to «interpret and transform» the given can be related to Lezama's insistence that new incongruous arrangements of image and metaphor offer new perceptions of reality, and new forms which after having been voiced start to demand substance. This demand for substance, an act of creation achieved by the agency of language, allows the language user to participate in the prerogatives of the divine in ways that are radically asserted by Juan Ramón in his statements of *Dios deseado y deseante,* particularly in «El nombre conseguido de los nombres», where by the power of naming, by the power of language, he becomes capable of creating and recreating the world, himself in the world, and God within himself and the world.

> Todos los nombres que yo puse
> al universo, que por ti me recreaba yo,
> se me están convirtiendo en uno y en un
> dios.
>
> El dios que es siempre al fin,
> el dios creado y recreado y recreado
> por gracia y sin esfuerzo.
> El Dios. El nombre conseguido de los nombres.
>
> (*LP,* p. 1292)

At this juncture, it could be argued that the main purpose of Juan Ramón's poetry becomes the expression and exploration of the blessed state of having achieved his mystical arrival, no longer primarily interested in the motions required to maintain his spiritual development. But even if his «camino mundo arriba» has taken him to a height where he can talk about achieving «sin esfuerzo», much of his emphasis still falls on the need repeatedly to reenact the pilgrimage towards this plentitude. The repetition of the verbs «crear» and «recrear», and the qualification of the «name of names» as «conseguido» rather than «dado», still stress the need to re-live both the creative motion, and the attendant succession of efforts exerted in order to *conseguir lo conseguido.*

The trajectory of Juan Ramón's spiritual development can be charted from every one of his personally revitalising discoveries to every one of his shared revitalising utterances, as a process of intensification of the habits of seeing, saying, salvaging. The process ascends all the way to the mystical extreme of identifying himself with the largest, and yet still ever-growing, manifestation of *conciencia* capable of creating and containing the fullness of a universe, indeed «fit for a god to inhabit».

Juan Ramón's insistence on «cómo el hombre puede ser hombre último con los dones que hemos supuesto a la divinidad encarnada, es decir enformada», demands, among so many other things, a reformulation of the Genesis account of Adam's stance before creation, and of Saint John's assertion concerning the primacy of the Word. The prerogatives hitherto attributed to the pre-existing Logos have to be devolved to a new Adam whose marvel will consist not in seeing the given for the first time, but in discovering that he gives himself the world he utters.

If the mystical synthesis of Juan Ramón Jiménez asked for a continued ascension of the individual towards the goal of becoming empowered with the attributes of the divine, his ethical and political demands suggest the adoption of a material simplicity that, without decreasing beauty, would facilitate the concentration of all efforts on the task of the desired ascent.

The ethical and political demands of Juan Ramón, as presented in his prose writing since 1936, can be seen as consonant with most ascetic programmes for reducing the material impediments to spiritual progress. Juan Ramón's «política poética» is important insofar as it denounces that kind of material progress which occasions more inhumanity than happiness, and insofar as it upholds the immensity of that minority of accomplished seekers and growers to whom he dedicates his labours. Even recognising the importance of his ethics and his politics, and their direct relevance to present global ethical and political issues, Juan Ramón's most significant contribution is still his insistence that poetry stands at the centre of any project of ethical, political or spiritual development.

Today, the most observable and empowered manifestations of the role of poetry in the creation of a new reality are to be found in the many projects of liberation, in which an image —always incongruous, always not viable— stands against the oppressive odds, and demands to be realised. Lezama's description of the last of his «Eras imaginarias» already defines a recently opened period of history in which an image itself has become the means and the end of liberation. Furthermore, if the people become poets in Lezama's sense of «guardianes de lo inexistente sustantivo», their habits of bringing into being the impossibles voiced by the image will create their new world. In accord with this, Vitier's conversion «de la conciencia de la poesía a la poesía de la conciencia» already represents the development of one individual creator from the habit of crafting *mots justes* on the page, to the habit of materialising those *palabras justas* in the world of the «real-izado».

In light of all this, it is important to realise the relevance of each individual's habits of *poeisis*. In a universe where death and entropy stand as incontrovertible facts, and in an economy where every unit of labour has the undesirable potential to degenerate into the profit and privilege of uncreative hands, every localised instance of order, justice, and life depends on an act of *poeisis*.

To conceive reality requires taking a stand within the following certainties: We can exist under the weight of the finality of death, the uselessness of suffering, and the inevitability of organic decay and entropic distention of atomic disorder. Or, we can live assured that the will keeps making energy available for work; that activity revitalises the bodies of the creatures while regeneration multiplies them; that —as Yeats says— there are ways of «transfiguring all that dread»; and that in some unmentionable way, the Resurrection may be a viable alternative.

If the ultimate validity of death and its attendant limitations become the rock-bottom bases of our metaphysics, the acts that issue from our vision are bound to be very few. Since all exertions would be inevitably subsumed in the final collapse, it would not be irresponsible to join the validated forces, and surrender from the onset to the paralysis of the radical nihilist. If, on the other hand, life, activity and regeneration become too much the evident foundation of the world, there is the danger of taking births, breaths and deeds for granted, to the point of developing an irresponsible stance towards life; a stance not dissimilar to the nihilist's paralysis.

Nevertheless, paying attention to the history of the world, and to the succession of processes that have occasioned our becoming, we are soon compelled to see all we know about that history and those processes as a more or less sustained expansion of geophysical stability and organic evolution, which, in fact, do not erradicate death, nor the ever-present tendencies towards disorder and decay.

As we insist on facing those facts, we should also reflect that in the long chain of related processes which account for our presence in the world there are a number which, despite how much we come to understand about their inception, will always strike us as leaps in which reality itself successfully attempted the impossible. The first collision of a pair of nuclei of heavy hydrogen to form a stable helium atom, the first concatenation of cellular events that ceased to be a mere chemical reaction to become a metabolic pathway, the first specific arrangement of nucleic acids which facilitated the perpetuation of a social contract, the first coincidence in the brain of word and thing; all represent instances in which substance and form was granted to the hitherto inexistent. Exercised against predominantly antivital tendencies, each of these miracles, and so many others, in time acquired the status of habits of creation. Soon they became fully orchestrated into the harmony of possible events which constitute normality, and from which spring the subsequent leaps toward the impossible.

This discussion of the habits of poetry practised and advocated by the four poets included in this presentation has tried to explore the ways in which poetry itself can be regarded as one of those miracles that become habits of creation: order-inducing utterance, life-making practice, matter-producing process, form-giving act. Poetry becomes fiat —created and creative habit within the created order.

> No está la muerte nuestra bajo tierra (...)
> Reviviremos hondos a más vida (...)
> Nos abrió una semilla y otra somos, y esto es sólo una vez; enjendrar más iguales no nos sigue, nos sigue una lengua inesperada.
> Lengua de nuestro mítico mudarnos en primavera; lengua de nuestro milagroso cumplimiento. ¿Una lengua de fuego, al fin poetas?
>
> *(Leyenda,* p. 636)

Poeisis, then, engages the development of habits of utterance to denominate every fresh instance of the miraculous deployment of reality, while at the same time imparting to reality an ever-increasing incidence of the miraculous. Language, like green leaves, and poetry, like photosynthesis, must habitually harness localised over-abundances of light and turn them into life, and nothing else.

LIST OF WORKS CONSULTED

ALBORNOZ, AURORA DE: «Juan Ramón Jiménez. Cuba. José Lezama Lima, y otros poetas cubanos», *Insula*, 36, nos. 416-17 (July-August 1981), p. 7.

ALBORNOZ, AURORA DE, ed.: *Juan Ramón Jiménez: El escritor y la crítica*. Madrid: Taurus, 1980.

BAEZA FLORES, ALBERTO: «Juan Ramón Jiménez y las Antillas Mayores», *Cuadernos Hispanoamericanos*, nos. 376-78 (October-December 1981), pp. 64-80.

BAQUERO, GASTÓN: «Juan Ramón vivo en el recuerdo», *Cuadernos Hispanoamericanos*, nos. 376-78 (October-December 1981), pp. 81-89.

BIANCHI ROSS, CIRO, ed.: «El momento cubano de Juan Ramón Jiménez: [por] José Lezama Lima, Fina García Marruz, y Cintio Vitier», *La Gaceta de Cuba*, no. 77 (October 1969), pp. 8-10.

COKE-ENGUÍDANOS, MERVYN: «Word and Work (with capital letters) in Juan Ramón Jiménez», *MLN*, 96, no. 2 (March 1982), pp. 224-36.

— *Word and Work in the Poetry of Juan Ramón Jiménez*. London: Tamesis, 1982.

COLE, LEO R.: *The Religious Instinct in the Poetry of Juan Ramón Jiménez*. Oxford: Dolphin, 1967.

CORTÁZAR, JULIO: *Rayuela*. Buenos Aires: Sudamericana, 1968.

— «Para llegar a Lezama Lima», *La vuelta al día en ochenta mundos*, 2 vols. Madrid: Siglo XXI, 1980.

D'AMBROSIO SERVODIDIO, MIRELLA: *The Quest for Harmony: The Dialectics of Communications in the Poetry of Eugenio Florit*. Lincoln, Neb.: Society of Spanish and Spanish American Studies, 1979.

DANTE: *Inferno*, Charles S. Singleton, trans., ed. Princeton: PUP, 1970.

DESNOES, EDMUNDO, ed.: *Los dispositivos en la flor. Cuba: Literatura desde la Revolución*. Hanover, N.H.: Ediciones del Norte, 1981.

DIEGO, ELISEO: «La opción de Lezama», *Granma* (resumen semanal), 18, no. 19. La Habana, 8 May 1983.

FLORIT, EUGENIO: «Una hora conmigo», *Revista Cubana*, 2, nos. 4-6 (1935), pages 159-67.

— *Poema mío*. México: Letras de México, 1947.

— «*Asonante final*» *y otros poemas*. La Habana: Orígenes, 1956.

— *Antología poética*. México: Ediciones de Andrea, 1956.

— *Hábito de esperanza*. Madrid: Insula, 1965.

— *Antología penúltima*. Madrid: Plenitud, 1970.

— *Poesía en José Martí, Juan Ramón Jiménez, Alfonso Reyes, Federico García y Pablo Neruda*. Miami: Universal, 1978.

— «La poesía de Juan Ramón Jiménez», *El escritor y la crítica*, A. de Albornoz, ed. Madrid: Taurus, 1980.

— *Obras completas*, vol. III, Luis González del Valle and Roberto Esquenazi-Mayo, eds. Lincoln, Neb.: Society of Spanish and Spanish American Studies, 1982.

FUZZOLARI, MARGARITA: *PARADISO y el sistema poético de José Lezama Lima.* Buenos Aires: García Gambeiro, 1979.

GARFIAS, FRANCISCO: «Juan Ramón Jiménez, escritor epistolar», *El escritor y la crítica,* A. de Albornoz, ed. Madrid: Taurus, 1980.

GUILLÉN, JORGE: *Cántico.* Barcelona: Barral, 1977.

GULLÓN, RICARDO: *Conversaciones con Juan Ramón Jiménez.* Madrid: Taurus, 1958.

— «El arte del retrato en Juan Ramón Jiménez», *El escritor y la crítica,* A. de Albornoz, ed. Madrid: Taurus, 1980.

HARVEY, VAN A.: *A Handbook of Theological Terms.* New York: Macmillan, 1964.

JIMÉNEZ, JUAN RAMÓN: «Prólogo: Estado poético cubano», *La poesía cubana en 1936,* José María Chacón y Calvo, Camila Henríquez Ureña, and Fernando Ortiz, eds. La Habana: Institución Hispanocubana de Cultura, 1937.

— «De mi 'Diario poético' 1936-37 (Fragmento)», *Revista Cubana,* 7, nos. 19-21 (January-March 1937), pp. 55-77.

— «Ciego ante ciegos», *Revista Cubana,* 10, nos. 28-30 (October-November 1937), pp. 35-51.

— «De mi 'Diario poético' 1936-37 (Fragmento)», *Universidad de la Habana,* no. 15 (November-December 1937), pp. 5-17.

— «De mi 'Diario poético' 1937-39 (Fragmento)», *Universidad de la Habana,* nos. 36-37 (May-August 1941), pp. 7-24.

— *La estación total, con las canciones de la nueva luz* (1923-1936). Buenos Aires: Losada, 1946.

— *Animal de fondo.* Buenos Aires: Pleamar, 1949.

— *Cuadernos de Juan Ramón Jiménez,* Francisco Garfias, ed. Madrid: Taurus, 1960.

— *La corriente infinita,* Francisco Garfias, ed. Madrid: Aguilar, 1961.

— *El trabajo gustoso (Conferencias),* Francisco Garfías, ed. México: Aguilar, 1961.

— *Libros de poesía,* Agustín Caballero, ed. Madrid: Aguilar, 1967.

— *Españoles de tres mundos,* Ricardo Gullón, ed. Madrid: Aguilar, 1969.

— *Tercera antolojía poética* (1898-1953), Eugenio Florit, ed. Madrid: Biblioteca Nueva, 1970.

— *En el otro costado,* A. de Albornoz, ed. Madrid: Ediciones Júcar, 1974.

— *Cartas literarias,* Francisco Garfias, ed. Barcelona: Bruguera, 1977.

— *Leyenda* (1896-1956), Antonio Sánchez Romeralo, ed. Madrid: Cupsa, 1978.

— *Isla de la simpatía,* Arcadio Díaz Quiñones and Raquel Sárraga, eds. Río Piedras: Hurracán, 1981.

— *Política poética,* Germán Bleiberg, ed. Madrid: Alianza Editorial, 1982.

LEZAMA LIMA, JOSÉ: «Gracia eficaz de Juan Ramón Jiménez y su visita a nuestra poesía», *Verbum,* 1, no. 3 (November 1937), pp. 57-64.

— ed.: *Verbum* (Organo oficial de la Asociación Nacional de Estudiantes de Derecho), 3 nos., La Habana: June, July-August, November, 1937.

— ed.: *Orígenes,* 40 nos., La Habana, 1944-56.

— *Antología de la poesía cubana.* La Habana: Editorial Consejo Nacional de Cultura, 1965.

— *Recopilación de textos sobre José Lezama Lima,* Pedro Simón Martínez, ed. La Habana: Casa de las Américas, 1970.

— *Obras completas,* vol. I, *Paradiso and Poesía,* intro. by Cintio Vitier. México: Aguilar, 1975.

— *Obras completas,* vol. II, *Ensayos y Cuentos.* México: Aguilar, 1977.

— *Cartas* (1939-1976), Eloísa Lezama Lima, ed. Madrid: Orígenes, 1979.

— *Paradiso,* Eloísa Lezama Lima, ed. Madrid: Cátedra, 1980.

LÓPEZ MORALES, HUMBERTO, ed., *Poesía contemporánea* (Antología). New York: Las Americas Publishing Co., 1967.

NERUDA, PABLO: *Confieso que he vivido.* Barcelona: Seix Barral, 1974.

O'CONNOR, FLANNERY: *The Habit of Being: The Letters of Flannery O'Connor.* New York: Vintage, 1980.

OLSON, PAUL R.: *Circle of Paradox: Time and Essence in the Poetry of Juan Ramón Jiménez.* Baltimore: JHUP, 1967.

PALAU DE NEMES, GRACIELA: *Vida y obra de Juan Ramón Jiménez.* Madrid: Gredos, 1957.

POUND, EZRA: *The Letters of Ezra Pound,* D. D. Paige, ed. London: Faber, 1950.

ROA, RAÚL: «Juan Ramón Jiménez», *El escritor y la crítica,* A. de Albornoz, ed. Madrid: Taurus, 1980.

RODRÍGUEZ PADRÓN, JORGE: «Juan Ramón Jiménez-Luis Cernuda: un diálogo crítico», *Cuadernos Hispanoamericanos,* nos. 376-78 (October-December 1981), pp. 886-910.

SAÍNZ, ENRIQUE, ed.: *La poesía cubana entre 1928 y 1958.* La Habana: Editorial Gente Nueva, 1980.

TILLICH, PAUL: *The Courage to Be.* New Haven: Yale, 1952.

UNAMUNO, MIGUEL DE: *Del sentimiento trágico de la vida.* Madrid: Selecciones Austral, 1976.

VALDIVIESO, JAIME: *Bajo el signo de Orfeo: Lezama Lima y Proust.* Madrid: Orígenes, 1980.

VITIER, CINTIO: «La poesía de Lezama Lima y el intento de una teleología insular», *Voces: Lezama Lima.* Barcelona: Montesinos Editor, undated.

— *Vísperas* (1938-1953). La Habana: Orígenes, 1953.

— *Testimonios* (1953-1968). La Habana: Contemporáneos, 1968.

— *Lo cubano en la poesía.* La Habana: Instituto del Libro, 1970.

— *Crítica sucesiva.* La Habana: Contemporáneos, 1971.

— *Poética.* Madrid: Giménez Arnáu Editor, 1973.

— *De Peña Pobre: memoria y novela.* México: Siglo XXI, 1978.

— «Homenaje a Juan Ramón Jiménez», *El escritor y la crítica,* A. de Albornoz, ed. Madrid: Taurus, 1980.

— «Cuba y la cultura latinoamericana» and «Entrevista», *Areíto,* 7, no. 27 (1981), pp. 7-10, 30-34.

— «Juan Ramón Jiménez en Cuba», *Sin Nombre,* 12, no. 3 (April-June 1982), pp. 31-56.

— «Nuestro Lezama», *Granma* (resumen semanal), 18, no. 10, 6 March 1983.

— ed. and co-author: *Diez poetas cubanos* (1937-1947). La Habana: Orígenes, 1948.

— ed.: *Juan Ramón Jiménez en Cuba.* La Habana: Arte y Literatura, 1981.

YOUNG, HOWARD T.: «The Exact Names», *MLN,* 96, no. 2 (March 1982), pages 212-23.